Management of Risk:
Guidance for Practitioners

Office of Government Commerce

London: TSO

The OGC is now the authority for best practice in commercial activities in UK Government, combining a number of separate functions with related aims.

OGC will build on the popular guidance developed by the former CCTA and others, working with organisations internationally to develop and share business and practitioner guidance within a world-class best practice framework.

Office of Government Commerce
IT Directorate
Rosebery Court
St Andrews Business Park
Norwich NR7 0HS
Service Desk: Telephone: 0845 000 4999
E-mail: info@ogc.gsi.gov.uk
Website: http://www.ogc.gov.uk/

First published 2002
Second impression 2003

ISBN 0 11 330909 0

Printed in the United Kingdom for The Stationery Office

CONTENTS

FOREWORD

Risk and risk management can sometimes be misunderstood. There is a view that the prudent approach is to avoid risk by simply maintaining the status quo. Linked to this is the idea that audit is a barrier to risk taking and innovation. Also spending time developing risk management strategies can sometimes be perceived as mere pointless bureaucracy.

Failure to take opportunities can be a huge risk in itself. By not looking at new ways of doing things organisations can miss out on real opportunities to manage better their business, improve service delivery and achieve value for money.

Following the Turnbull report organisations are now busy working on risk management frameworks and internal control statements to embed risk management in their management processes.

This publication draws on experience from a variety of experts from the public and private sectors. It sets out a framework for taking informed decisions about risk at a project, programme and strategic level to ensure that key risks are identified, assessed and that action is taken to address them.

This guidance should be a valuable springboard for innovation and encourage a sound approach to risk.

Michael Whitehouse

Assistant Auditor General, National Audit Office

![NAO NATIONAL AUDIT OFFICE]

ACKNOWLEDGEMENTS

The contributions of Kelvin Lack and Steve Daniels of Insight Consulting, and Jane Chittenden of Format Ltd, under contract to OGC, are acknowledged as significant in the design and development of the practical content of this guidance.

OGC would also like to thank the following individuals and organisations for their contributions and support throughout the design and development of the M_o_R guidance.

Tony Betts	OGC
Martin Carr	OGC
Chris Groom	NAO
David Cronin	Dartmouth Park Systems
Michael Dallas	David Langdon & Everest
Carole Edrich	KAI Corporation (Risk)
Val Jonas	Risk Decisions
Eric Mahy	Line International
Rosemary Mulley	Nabarro Nathanson
Pippa Newman	independent consultant
Ian Robertson	OGC
Brian Stowger	Ampleford Strategic Consultants Ltd
Owen Wright	CSE

In particular, Frances Scarff, the OGC Project Manager and technical contributor, would like to express special thanks to all delegates at the workshops on management of risk which were held as part of our programme to respond to the recommendations of the 'Successful IT: Modernising Government in Action' report. In total there were over 50 attendees and all their contributions were welcome in validating the scope and design of the guidance.

OGC is in the process of registering the trademark M_o_R ™.

1

CHAPTER 1: INTRODUCTION

1.1 Purpose of this guide

This guide is intended to help organisations to put in place effective frameworks for taking informed decisions about risk. The guidance provides a route map for risk management, bringing together recommended approaches, checklists and pointers to more detailed sources of advice on tools and techniques. It expands on the OGC Guidelines for Managing Risk.

The process of investment appraisal, in which assessments are made of costs, benefits and risks, is outside the scope of this guide. However, many of the principles and techniques described here can be used when developing the business case. The approach described in this guide complements OGC's guidance on programme and project management and is continually updated to reflect current thinking. This approach, branded by OGC as M_o_R (Management of Risk), is supported by training and qualifications.

1.2 What is management of risk?

In this guide risk is defined as *uncertainty of outcome*, whether positive opportunity or negative threat. The term 'management of risk' incorporates all the activities required to identify and control the exposure to risk which may have an impact on the achievement of an organisation's business objectives.

Every organisation manages its risk, but not always in a way that is visible, repeatable and consistently applied to support decision making. The task of management of risk is to ensure that the organisation makes cost effective use of a risk process that has a series of well defined steps. The aim is to support better decision making through a good understanding of risks and their likely impact.

There are two distinct phases: risk analysis and risk management. Risk analysis is concerned with gathering information about exposure to risk so that the organisation can make appropriate decisions and manage risk appropriately.

Management of risk involves having processes in place to monitor risks, access to reliable and up to date information about risks, the right balance of control in place to deal with those risks, and decision making processes supported by a framework of risk analysis and evaluation.

Management of risk covers a wide range of topics, including business continuity management, security, programme/project risk management and operational service management. These topics need to be placed in the context of an organisational framework for the management of risk. Some risk-related topics, such as security, are highly specialised and this guidance provides only an overview of such aspects.

1.3 Why management of risk is important

A certain amount of risk taking is inevitable if your organisation is to achieve its objectives. Effective management of risk helps you to improve performance by contributing to:

- increased certainty and fewer surprises

- better service delivery

- more effective management of change

- more efficient use of resources

- better management at all levels through improved decision making

- reduced waste and fraud, and better value for money

- innovation

- management of contingent and maintenance activities.

See Annex A for examples of the benefits of more effective management of risk.

1.4 Who is involved in risk management

In practice, everyone in an organisation is involved in risk management to some extent and should be aware of their responsibilities in identifying and managing risk. However, there are some aspects for which responsibility must be assigned to individuals. Without clear responsibility (and the authority to support that responsibility) some risks will be missed or overlooked.

In the public sector, there are two major roles with a clear responsibility to ensure risks are managed (there will be equivalents to these roles in private sector organisations). These roles are:

- an Accounting Officer (or equivalent senior manager), who is responsible for the organisation's overall exposure to risk. Typically this person will be the Chief Executive Officer (CEO); the senior manager in the organisation. They may delegate some of the actions but cannot forgo the responsibility

- a senior manager acting as a project 'owner', who is responsible for risk relating to a specific programme or project and for the realisation of associated business benefits.

Audience for this guidance

Business managers, process owners, strategic planners, project and procurement teams, business continuity planners and security teams are the primary audience for this guidance, together with their service providers.

It will also be of interest to auditors, with their responsibility for ensuring effective corporate governance.

1.5   How to use this guide

Chapter 1 introduces the structure, process and culture of management of risk, explaining why organisations need to devise and implement effective strategies in order to maximise opportunities and minimise threats to the achievement of their business objectives. It identifies key personnel in the management of risk and the target audience for the guidance.

Chapter 2 outlines the key principles underpinning management of risk: establishing a risk management framework, risk ownership, where risks occur, the decision making process, the importance of embedding the risk management culture, and allocating realistic budgets.

Chapter 3 describes the main activities of management of risk. It contains practical examples, pointers and checklists for identifying and responding to risk, and monitoring risk responses.

Chapters 4–7 explain when and how management of risk should be applied throughout an organisation, at the strategic, programme, project and operational levels.

Chapter 8 discusses the range of techniques available to support the risk management process.

The Annexes provide supporting detail:

- A: Examples of benefits of risk management

- B: Healthcheck: how well is your organisation managing risk?

- C: Categorising risk

- D: Setting a standard for evaluation of risk

- E: Procurement, contractual and legal considerations

- F: Business continuity management

- G: Managing organisational safety and security

- H: Information on further techniques to support management of risk

- J: Lessons learned from others

- K: Assessing the suitability of tools

- L: Documentation outlines.

1.6   The research for this guidance

Prepared by OGC's IT Directorate, this guidance has been developed from extensive research into current thinking and practice in both the public and private sectors, drawing on published papers and interviews/studies with a number of leading organisations involved in major change and with specialist experts in the management of risk. It builds on the recent work of the National Audit Office (NAO), HM Treasury and Cabinet Office, together with OGC's published guidance on best practice in risk management; it also aims to address issues relating to corporate governance.

This guidance responds to lessons learned and the experiences of real-world practical issues, as reported by consultants in OGC's Strategic Assignments Consultancy Service and their clients. In addition, it incorporates feedback from contributors to OGC workshops and other review channels. These contributions are acknowledged with thanks.

2

CHAPTER 2: PRINCIPLES

This chapter outlines the key principles underpinning the effective management of risk.

2.1 Critical success factors for management of risk

The key elements that need to be in place if risk management is to be effective, and innovation encouraged, include:

- clearly identified senior management to support, own and lead on risk management

- risk management policies and the benefits of effective management clearly communicated to all staff

- existence and adoption of a framework for management of risk that is transparent and repeatable

- existence of an organisational culture which supports well thought-through risk taking and innovation

- management of risk fully embedded in management processes and consistently applied

- management of risk closely linked to achievement of objectives

- risks associated with working with other organisations explicitly assessed and managed

- risks actively monitored and regularly reviewed on a constructive 'no-blame' basis.

Joint working and partnerships often involve more complex types of risk that can adversely affect the delivery of business services. For example, if part of the service provided by one organisation is delayed or of poor quality, the success of the whole collaboration can be put at risk. You must make sure that your organisation knows about the risk management approaches of your partners. Sharing information about risk management means that risks in collaborative programmes can be identified and managed in a proactive way.

Public sector concerns

The Modernising Government initiative seeks to encourage the public sector to adopt well managed risk taking where it is likely to lead to sustainable improvements in service delivery. More effective risk management will improve the public sector's ability to undertake the increasingly complex and cross-cutting projects that are demanded by the Modernisation agenda. Public sector organisations need to have in place the skills, management structures and organisational structures to take advantage of potential opportunities to perform better and to reduce the possibility of failure.

The key areas that have to be addressed are:

- the requirements of corporate governance – including more focused and open ways of managing risk (see the section on corporate governance below)

- the need for a 'risk owner' at senior level, for an activity (strategy, programme or project). He or she is supported by risk owners at everyday working levels as appropriate for the activity and risk exposure

- the need for improved reporting and upward referral of major problems

- opportunities and the potential resolution approaches

- the need for shared understanding of risk management at all levels in the organisation and with partners, combined with consistent treatment of risk

- managing project risk in the wider context of programmes of change and the business.

The NAO study of risk management (*Supporting Innovation: Managing Risk in Government Departments*), the Cabinet Office's report *Successful IT: Modernising Government in Action*, and HM Treasury's *Orange Book* provide valuable messages that are incorporated in this guidance.

Meeting the needs of corporate governance

Corporate governance is the ongoing activity of maintaining a sound system of internal control to safeguard shareholders' investment and the company's assets.

The Turnbull Report states that:

> 'a company's objectives, its internal organisation and the environment which it operates in are continually evolving and as a result the risks it faces are continually changing. A sound system of control therefore depends on a thorough and regular evaluation of the nature and extent of the risks to which the company is exposed. Since profits [or business results] are in part the reward for successful risk taking in business, the purpose of internal control is to help manage and control risk rather than eliminate it.'

Corporate governance frameworks must ensure that management is held accountable for a corporation's performance and that owners are able to monitor and intervene in the operations of management.

These principles apply equally to the public and private sectors. Whereas corporations focus mainly on shareholder returns and the preservation of shareholders' value, the public sector's role is to implement programmes cost effectively in accordance with Government legislation and policies.

The British Standards Institute (BSI) has produced a guidance note on *Corporate Governance – PD 6668:2000* – relating to the management of strategic risks. It outlines a management framework for identifying the threats, determining the risks, implementation and maintaining control measures and finally reporting annually on the organisation's commitment to this process.

Policy on management of risk to support corporate governance

To support corporate governance, there needs to be a risk management policy in place. This policy should:

- be appropriate for the size and nature of your organisation, its business and operating environment

- be clear about the roles (and, if possible, individuals) that are responsible for risk

- be clear about escalation criteria in relation to risk management (i.e., when to refer decision making upwards)

- ensure that processes, and the culture/infrastructure, to identify and manage risk are put in place; these processes must be repeatable

- set up the mechanism for monitoring the success of the application of the policy (including reports to management, at least annually)

- ensure that internal control mechanisms are in place for independent assessment that the policy is implemented (and checked).

2.2   What is at risk and why?

There are many diverse factors that could place an organisation at risk. Figure 1 outlines the main reasons why there should be a robust risk management process in place.

Your organisation will have a set of key objectives. Risks should be identified against these objectives, ideally not more than 10-15 at high level. These high-level risks will then be considered and managed by senior management, increasing the organisation's ability to meet its objectives. Annex B provides a 'healthcheck' to see if an organisation is adopting an effective framework for management of risk and risk management process.

Annex C expands on possible categories of risk.

Relating management of risk to safety, security and business continuity

Management of risk should be carried out in the wider context of safety concerns, security and business continuity.

- Health and safety policy and practice is concerned with ensuring that the workplace is a safe environment.

- Security is concerned with protecting the organisation's assets, including information, buildings and so on.

- Business continuity is concerned with ensuring that the organisation could continue to operate in the event of a disaster, such as loss of a service, flood or fire damage.

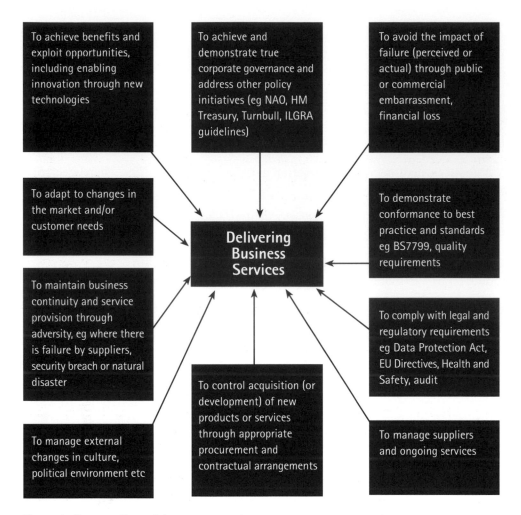

Figure 1: Reasons for a risk management process

Reducing risk in large scale projects

Experience has shown that programmes and projects attempting a large scale, comprehensive business change are less likely to be successful than those taking a less ambitious, step-by-step approach. Although the latter increases management activity, with each of the elements needing to be controlled and coordinated, the advantages are that activities are:

- easier to manage
- simpler to implement within the business environment
- easier to accept formally as, typically, the specification is easier to document and thus simpler to verify that it has been met
- able to offer more options for contingency
- more likely to accommodate fast moving changes in technology, or in the political or financial environment
- able to offer more decision points, allowing greater control of the project.

2.3 Decisions about risk

Decisions about risk need to be balanced so that the potential benefits are worth more to the organisation than it costs to address the risk.

For example, innovation is inherently risky but could achieve major benefits in improving services. The ability of the organisation to limit its exposure to risk will also be of relevance.

You should aim to make an accurate assessment of the risks in a given situation and analyse the potential benefits. The risks and opportunities presented by each course of action should be defined in order to identify appropriate response.

Scope of decisions

Decisions about risk will vary depending on whether the risk relates to long, medium or short-term goals.

Strategic decisions are primarily concerned with long-term goals; these set the context for decisions at other levels of the organisation. The risks associated with strategic decisions may not become apparent until well into the future. Thus it is essential to review these decisions, and associated risks, on a regular basis.

Medium-term goals are usually addressed through programmes and projects to bring about business change. Decisions relating to medium-term goals are narrower in scope than strategic ones, particularly in terms of timeframe and financial responsibilities.

At the operational level the emphasis is on short-term goals to ensure ongoing continuity of business services; however, decisions about risk at this level must also support the achievement of long- and medium-term goals. These organisational levels are discussed in more detail in Chapters 4, 5, 6 and 7.

There are also considerations about what can realistically be achieved in one change initiative. Delivery of each of the components of a change initiative (whether a programme, project or stage) must provide some direct benefit to the organisation as a result of its delivery. This could be by delivering:

- a major component to support/build towards the intended outcome – for example, providing a telephone helpline first as part of a new information service and then adding website services to expand the facilities available to the public

- the product to part of the end user community and then 'rolling out' to the rest of that community – for example, introducing a new information service in the North-East and gradually making it available nationwide.

This is a modular and/or incremental approach that is further discussed in Chapters 5 and 6 and in Annex E.

When managing any project it is essential to ensure major decisions are made appropriately. A project will support some business change and so require something to be produced and then put into use.

Figure 2 shows the main stages of the procurement process and the decisions to be taken about breaking projects down into manageable 'packages'. For major projects, there will be formal Gateway Reviews in addition to the normal project decision points; these reviews establish whether the project is ready to proceed to the next stage.

The acquisition lifecycle

The key stages below assume a procurement for a project. However, the principles can be adapted to any type of project where a full business case process is required, including cross-cutting projects

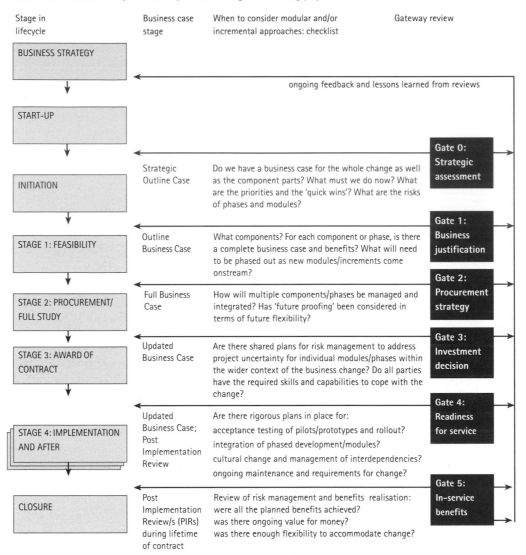

Figure 2: Main stages of the procurement process

2.4   Where risks occur

The risk management process should be most rigorously applied where critical decisions are being made.

Figure 3 shows where risk can occur in an organisation. For convenience, these levels are described as:

● strategic or corporate

● programme

- project

- operational.

In practice, the levels overlap; however, it is helpful to clarify the occurrence of risks at these levels to inform the kind of decisions you are likely to make.

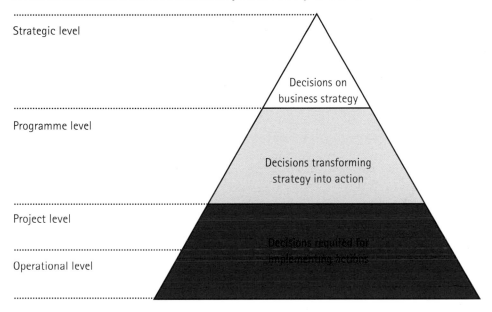

Figure 3: Organisational management hierarchy

It is important to note that a risk may materialise initially at one level but subsequently have a major impact at a different level. A recent example is a High Street bank facing technical faults at the operational level; ultimately customers' confidence in the bank's online service became a strategic risk. This highlights the need for relevant information about risks to be shared throughout the organisation.

Table 1 shows examples of typical risks occurring at each organisational level.

Table 1: Risk related to organisational levels

Level	Examples of typical risks considered at this level
Strategic/corporate	Commercial, financial, political, environmental, directional, cultural, acquisition and quality risks. There is a focus on business survival, continuity and growth for the future. When programme, project and operational risks exceed set criteria – e.g. not acceptable, outside agreed limits, could affect strategic objectives, information needs to be escalated to this level so that appropriate decisions can be taken.
Programme	Procurement/acquisition, funding, organisational, projects, security, safety, quality and business continuity risks. When project and operational risks exceed set criteria – e.g. not acceptable, outside agreed limits, could affect programme objectives, information needs to be escalated to this level so that appropriate decisions can be taken.

Level	Examples of typical risks considered at this level
Project	Personal, technical, cost, schedule, resource, operational support, quality and provider failure. Operational issues/risks should be considered at this level as they affect the project and how it needs to be run. Information on strategic and programme related risks should be communicated to this level where they could affect project objectives. Project managers should communicate information on risks to other projects and operations as appropriate.
Operations	Personal, technical, cost, schedule, resource, operational support, quality, provider failure, environmental and infrastructure failure. All the higher levels have input to this level; specific concerns include business continuity management/contingency planning, support for business processes and customer relations.

Additional factors

Additional factors may increase the complexity of assessing overall exposure to risk. These include:

- interdependencies, or links between projects and/or related issues, where the impact of one or more risks could affect others, possibly creating a 'domino' effect. You should ensure that any known interdependencies are identified and assessed so that appropriate action can be planned

- the relationship between business benefits and risks to delivery, where achievement of benefits is dependent on successful delivery of a project. You should continually check whether changing plans affect the achievement of benefits.

2.5   A framework for managing risk

A framework for management of risk sets the context in which risks will be identified, analysed, controlled, monitored and reviewed. It must be consistent with processes that are embedded in everyday management and operational practices. It addresses:

- how risks are identified

- how information about their probability and potential impact is obtained

- how risks are quantified

- how options to deal with them are identified

- how decisions on risk management are made, such as further risk reduction

- how these decisions are implemented

- how actions are evaluated for their effectiveness

- how appropriate communication mechanisms are set up and supported

- how stakeholders are engaged throughout the process.

(See Chapter 3 for more information about the management of risk framework and supporting processes.)

2.6   Risk ownership

For the organisation, ownership of the risk management framework lies with the Accounting Officer (or equivalent senior manager at Board level). Individual senior managers own the programme or project and are responsible for the management of the overall risk of that activity. However, these roles do not own all the individual risks. Risk ownership must be clearly defined, documented and agreed with the individual owners at all levels, so that they understand their various roles, responsibilities and ultimate accountability with regard to the management of risk. The owner of a risk may not be the person tasked with the assessment or management of the risk, but he or she is responsible for ensuring the management of risk process is applied – there may be separate owners to actually deal with the risks.

It is important to identify who owns:

- the setting policy and the organisation's willingness to take risk

- the management of risk process at the different levels – that is, strategic, programme, project, operational levels

- different elements of the management of risk process, such as identifying threats, through to producing risk responses and reporting on decisions

- implementation of the actual measures taken in response to the risks

- interdependent risks that cross organisational boundaries, whether they are business processes, operational services or projects.

For example, for a senior manager with responsibility for a project, ownership of risk could be defined as follows:

> Senior managers responsible for projects must assure themselves that a number of types of risk are being tracked and dealt with as effectively as possible. The mechanisms in place for monitoring and reporting risk will vary according to the size and complexity of the project or programme, ranging from the use of a simple risk register to the appointment of a risk manager reporting directly to the senior manager. Clearly, the degree of delegation adopted by the senior manager will vary, but he or she must be sure that the critical issues are being addressed; for example, through chairing the project board or by developing strong mechanisms for reporting problems.

Checklist: ownership of risk and the process

- Have owners been allocated for all the various parts of the complete management of risk process?

- Are the various roles and responsibilities associated with ownership well defined?

- Do the individuals who have been allocated ownership actually have the authority and capability to fulfil their responsibilities? For example, suppliers may be tasked with risk ownership.

- Have the various roles and responsibilities been communicated and understood?

- Are the nominated owners appropriate and aware of their nomination?

- Is ownership reassessed on a periodic basis, or in the event of a change in the situation; and if necessary, can it be quickly and effectively reallocated?

- Do all risks, and where appropriate their mitigation actions, have clearly identified owners? Are these owners appropriate?

2.7   Embedding the risk management culture

Identifying appropriate policies, standards and practices is the first stage of creating a risk management culture. Once these are in place they need to be totally embedded in individuals through the enactment of their roles and associated responsibilities.

Awareness of and responsibility for risk issues must be linked explicitly to key objectives, in order to build a sustainable risk management culture. There should be delegated responsibility for risks at every level of objectives in the organisation. This is the major support to embedding risk management into the organisation and its culture, with risk management seen as an intrinsic part of the way an organisation works. As the people in an organisation change, it is essential to ensure a continuing understanding of roles and responsibilities related to managing risk.

The risk environment is constantly changing too. Your organisation's priorities and the relative importance of risks will shift and change. Assumptions about risk have to be regularly revisited and reconsidered, perhaps by annual review of the risks associated with each of the key organisational objectives.

Establishing appropriate competencies and behaviours

An important aspect of setting up a risk culture is to ensure it is relevant to the organisation. Risk management is a major facet of effective corporate governance.

Those responsible for corporate governance need to have knowledge and understanding of:

- strategic planning

- legal requirements

- agreements and contracts

- communication techniques and information management

- staff matters, including how staff can be motivated and involved

- education opportunities and continual professional development

- continuous improvement and/or analytical techniques

- how the organisation is monitored and evaluated

- resource management, including equal opportunities and delegation.

Although managers tend to work in specific areas of the organisation, either based on technical specialism or business function, they all need to identify and manage risk. To do this they need to be able to:

- ensure that the situation is properly scoped

- identify and assess the risk

- create valid options for reducing risk to an acceptable level

- collect appropriate and meaningful information to assess risk and the options, and then to monitor the risk

- use sound reasoning when making a trade-off between the costs and benefits of managing a risk

- make a clear commitment to a particular course of action.

For planning, the major areas to consider are:

- deciding on the likelihood of a specific event occurring

- prioritising areas to address/actions to instigate. This requires understanding the implications of the options available

- assigning ownership of risks and actions, containment or contingent, to be deployed in a timely manner

- ensuring that continuity plans can cope with the current and potential future situation, not with how things were in the recent past.

Visible information on risk

Information on risk and its management needs to reach the people who have to take action or make decisions. This information will flow downwards and upwards between the organisational levels. There will also be sideways flows across each level, between programmes or projects. The vertical flows are the most important as they reflect levels of responsibility for decision making.

For example, a decision may be made at the strategic level that affects the progress of current programmes. Conversely, the collective risks relating to the progress of current programmes may have a strategic impact.

These examples illustrate why risks should be identified and handled at each level before they are passed up or down to the next level. Good communication mechanisms are essential to avoid the following problems:

- inadequate communication from lower levels, where people have 'hands on' knowledge, to the level where decisions are made, leads to unrealistic expectations from senior management

- inadequate communication from the top down can mean that projects are no longer supporting the business direction.

Communications

To address these problems you will need to ensure that appropriate communication mechanisms exist and are adopted. Your organisation should:

- ensure there is sufficient communication to key stakeholders, whether internal or external, to support their needs

- ensure that people are aware, informed and understand their part in managing risk

- consider whether there is a need to improve internal communications

- consider training needs and how these can be met adequately
- ensure people have the right information at the right time to fulfil their responsibilities (and how to recognise if this does not happen).

See Chapter 8 for more information on Risk Registers and Summary Risk Profiles.

Ensuring that your controls are adequate

There must be adequate control mechanisms to meet the needs of corporate governance. These will be described in the risk policy and implemented through the risk management framework. Specific controls will be introduced across the organisation to cope with certain circumstances, such as through the use of programme and project management.

Once an appropriate set of controls is adopted, an independent audit will check that they are in place, adequate and in use.

2.8   Budgets

The management of risk process must be embedded in the organisation, rather than being tacked on as an afterthought. The cost of carrying out the process will depend upon the technical, political and organisational complexity involved, but it needs to be recognised, with budgets agreed and allocated. Elements to be costed include:

- development, maintenance and dissemination of the risk policy
- creation and maintenance of the supporting infrastructure for use across the organisation (including the acquisition of support tools)
- development and/or acquisition of relevant skills (including training)
- loss of business capability while implementing new processes to manage risk.

Experience has shown that when planning projects and programmes you should expect to spend 1–3% of your budget on an initial risk analysis and management effort, and an additional 2% on updating this throughout the development lifecycle.

Operational units need to develop and maintain a number of plans relating to ensuring service continuity. Major elements include information security, contingency and business continuity planning. Thus, typically, operational units need to spend 10–30 % of their budget on risk related activities.

3

CHAPTER 3: HOW RISKS ARE MANAGED

This chapter explains the main components of the risk management process. In summary, the process involves:

- identifying risks in relation to key objectives

- evaluating risks to establish:

    ▪ the probability of those risks occurring

    ▪ the potential impact if they did occur

    ▪ your attitude to those risks in terms of willingness to accept them or not (looking at individual risks and the organisation's overall exposure to risk)

- deciding what to do about them – transfer them, tolerate them, treat them or terminate them

- monitoring the situation (reporting on and reviewing it to give ongoing assurance).

3.1   Defining a framework for management of risk

The minimum requirements for a management of risk framework are:

- establishment of the risk policy

- identification, and when appropriate, assignment of risk owners from among the stakeholders

- definition and adoption of suitable approaches for identifying risks; assessing risks and reporting them; action to deal with risks

- definition of responsibilities for managing risk and reporting to senior management, especially risks which cut across core business activities and organisational boundaries

- establishment of quality assurance (QA) arrangements to ensure that risk management reflects current good practice.

Figure 4 shows a strategic framework for the management of risk, and the processes are outlined throughout this chapter.

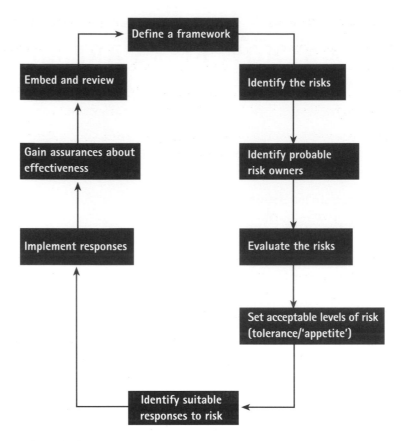

Adapted from the HM Treasury Orange Book

Figure 4: Strategic framework for the management of risk

Process to define a risk management framework

The process objective is:

- to define or validate the risk management policy to be adopted to ensure an adequate management of risk framework exists to address the relevant activity.

The process activities to define a risk management policy are outlined below.

- Identify relevant standards, policies and legal requirements.

- Identify (or validate) the context and perspective for the situation (e.g. What level of the organisation are we at? Which stakeholders' views are of primary importance?).

- Agree (or validate) management of risk objectives, constraints and concerns.

- Establish how a successful outcome is to be judged.

- Identify the tools and techniques to be adopted.

- Identify scale for evaluation of risk (see Section 3.6 and Annex D).

- Document the above in the risk policy reflecting the current situation and how the management of risk framework is supported.

Practical pointers for defining the risk management policy are listed below.

- The risk management policy needs to be clear and show how management of risk is to be adopted within the situation (and any associated plan).

- Tools and techniques to be adopted will clarify skills required and so reflect resource requirements. These should be realistic for the task in hand.

- Techniques to be adopted must be appropriate to support identification and subsequent management and tracking.

3.2   Risk identification

At a high level, you will focus on identifying the key risks to successful achievement of organisational objectives. These are the risks that are most likely to affect your performance and delivery of business services. At a lower level you will be looking in detail at the risks affecting programmes, projects and operational services.

Identified risks are usually held in a 'Risk Register' or Risk Log (an example is shown in Section 3.8). Chapters 4-7 investigate the specific risks associated with those levels; Chapter 8 and Annex H outline some techniques for identifying risks.

There is often confusion about the difference between a threat and a risk. A threat is a factor that could lead to a risk occurring, i.e. will be the cause of a risk. For example, there is a general threat of shortage of skilled project managers. If that threat becomes reality in an organisation, there is a consequent risk that the project team may not have adequate skills and experience.

Another area of confusion is between risk and issue. An issue is a concern that cannot be avoided, such as an unrealistic timescale for delivering a project, whereas a risk may not actually materialise. Once the issue has been identified, it can be managed appropriately.

When identifying risks you may find that you also identify possible measures (that is, courses of action) for addressing them. These measures should not influence you at this stage, as some may themselves present risks.

One widely used approach for identifying risks is to break them down into categories, which can then be used as a prompt list for identifying your organisation's main areas of risk. For example:

- strategic/commercial risks
- economic/financial/market risks
- legal, contractual and regulatory risks
- organisational management/human factors
- political/societal factors
- environmental factors/Acts of God (force majeure)
- technical/operational/infrastructure risks.

Process to identify the risks

The process objective is:

- to create or refine a Risk Register to record the currently identified risks.

The process activities to identify risks are:

- Gather or update information on possible risks (threats).

- Consider opportunities and how these are affected.

- Group risks (initially) according to where they have been identified.

Practical pointers for identifying risks are listed below.

- Sub-dividing the situation into a set of activities or products will help to make it manageable. Even the most complex situation should not involve more than 35 major activities or products.

- List possible threats (causes of risk) for the situation as a whole. Some threats will be more significant than others. See Annex C for more information on categories and causes of risk.

- Identify all the threats. Any threat not identified will lead to a risk that is not being actively managed or monitored and so is, in effect, accepted.

- Consider opportunities to support the vision for the future. Each opportunity is likely to have associated risk which must be considered and included in the risk register.

- Consider stakeholder viewpoints as their views on what poses a threat or signifies success will vary and need to be understood.

- Think 'outside the box'.

Checklist on risk identification

- Has a clear policy on the application of a risk-oriented management process and the scope of risks to be addressed been set at the appropriate level?

- Has the scope for management of risk been directly linked to the context and objectives of the situation?

- Has this been agreed and clearly communicated from the outset?

- Is the risk policy reviewed regularly to ensure it is still appropriate – that is, are strategic objectives linked to those of the programmes, projects and operations?

- Have changes to the objectives of the situation been fed back into the risk process and linked back to the entries in the risk register?

- Does the management of risk process cater for all different types of risk?

- Has a full, comprehensive set of threats been identified? Can you demonstrate this?

- Has a range of appropriate identification approaches been adopted?

- Has an appropriate set of tools and techniques been identified and adopted for managing risk?

20

3.3   Identifying probable risk owners

At this point in the process it should be possible to look at the identified threats and identify people who could be tasked with owning them.

Ownership itself will not be assigned until after the extent of the risk is understood and the responses that are to be adopted are known. However, it is useful to consider who might be available to take on ownership, as that may affect how the threat can be treated.

Process to identify probable risk owners

The process objective is

- to identify possible risk owners from within the stakeholders, for each threat so far identified.

The process activities are:

- Identify or validate who the stakeholders are.

- For each threat, identify possible risk owners.

- Assess their potential to accept the responsibility.

- Update risk register with this information.

A practical pointer for this process is:

- some threats may have several potential owners; all practical choices should be documented at this point.

3.4   Risk evaluation

Risk evaluation is concerned with assessing probability and impact of individual risks, taking into account any interdependencies or other factors outside the immediate scope under investigation:

- Probability is the evaluated likelihood of a particular threat or event actually happening, including a consideration of the frequency with which this may arise.

- Impact is the evaluated effect or result of a particular risk actually happening.

For example, there is only a small risk of major damage to a building, but there would be enormous impact on business continuity were it to occur; conversely, the risk of an occasional system failure, such as IT or telecoms, is high but this would not normally have a major impact on the business.

Some types of risk, such as financial risk, can be evaluated in numerical terms; others, such as adverse publicity, can only be evaluated in subjective ways. You will need to develop a framework for categorising risks, as (say) very high, high, medium, low, very low, as shown in Table 2.

You will also need to gain a clear understanding of the risks and their interactions, as well as the potential complications created by some possible responses (whether containment or contingent).

It is vital to understand that risks are time based, not constant. Their occurrence will be due at particular times and the severity of their impact will vary depending on when they occur. This time factor is called the 'proximity' of the risk. Knowing when the threats present a greater risk will help identify the appropriate response and the required trigger and timing of the response.

Table 2: Example of risk probability framework

Probability	Criteria
Very low	0–5% (extremely unlikely, or virtually impossible)
Low	6–20% (low but not impossible)
Medium	21–50% (fairly likely to occur)
High	51%–80% (more likely to occur than not)
Very high	>80% (almost certainly will occur)

There are many ways in which risks can be evaluated (see Annex D). One of the most widely used is risk profiling (see Chapter 8: Techniques).

Process to evaluate the risks

The process objectives are:

- to determine the probability, impact and proximity (timing) of the identified threats
- where appropriate, to sort risks based on their importance (criticality).

The process activities are:

- Assess qualitatively (based on scale documented in risk policy) each of the identified threats in terms of probability, impact and proximity.
- Assess need to adopt qualitative analysis (for some or all risks).
- Undertake quantitative risk assessment if appropriate.
- Update Risk Register details.
- Sort risks in order of priority.

Practical pointers are listed below.

- Only use quantitative analysis if the additional information forms an important support to decisions on responding to threat. The validity of qualitative analysis is directly related to several factors including:
  - the accuracy of historical information
  - the bias and inexperience of personnel
  - ambiguity over the terms of reference for the analysis.
- While it is important to analyse each risk individually, it is essential to look for dependencies between risks (either threats or impacts).

- Risks that have very high probability and impact must be addressed. Lesser risks may be less critical and some may be accepted as they are. Generally the top 10-15 risks are analysed further, but all risks should be retained on the Risk Register and monitored to retain control (bearing in mind the resources available and whether the exposure justifies the associated costs).

- Identification and evaluation of technical risks needs to be completed early to ensure that all potential resolution options are opened up. Correcting problems later in the process is generally more costly and difficult.

3.5   Setting risk tolerances

The amount of risk your organisation is prepared to tolerate, or its 'risk appetite', will vary according to the perceived importance of particular risks and the timing (it may be more open to risk at different points in time). You may be prepared to take comparatively large risks in some areas and none at all in others. For example, your view of financial risks and how much the organisation is prepared to put at risk will depend on a number of variables such as budgets, the effect on other parts of the organisation, or additional risks such as political embarrassment.

To establish the optimum balance of a risk occurring against the costs and value for money of limiting that risk, you have to consider perceptions of tolerance in detail. Some organisations are willing to take more risk than others. These cultural aspects will assist in setting the risk tolerance level.

Once this is established, senior managers can decide on risk tolerance levels for individual programmes and projects, dictating when information about risk has to be referred upwards.

Process to set acceptable levels of risk

The process objective is:

- to determine the overall level of risk which the organisation can tolerate for the given situation.

The process activities are:

- Check whether the 'risk tolerance level' is preset within the risk policy, or identify the appropriate level.

- Gain management agreement to the risk tolerance level.

- Document appropriately (could be as part of the introductory information to the Risk Register or as part of the risk policy – wherever it would be most appropriate).

Practical pointers are listed below.

- The risk tolerance level is the maximum overall exposure to risk that should be accepted, based on the benefits and costs involved.

- If the responses to risk cannot bring the risk exposure to below this level, the activity must be referred upwards and will probably need to be stopped.

- Where personnel are less experienced, your organisation is likely to tolerate less exposure to risk.

- The 'risk tolerance line' can be drawn on the Summary Risk Profile (see Chapter 8: Techniques). Anything above and right of the line has to be referred upwards and may cause activity to cease.

Checklist: risk evaluation and assessment of the organisation's willingness to take on risk

- Has the level of analysis that is required to support the decision process been agreed from the outset, such as start of the project, acquisition lifecycle etc?

- Is there a demonstrable correlation between the amount of time, effort and cost expended in risk analysis to the difficulty in obtaining decisions, resources and funding for risk management etc?

- Is the level of analysis, where possible, commensurate with the level of risk? For example, are detailed assessments of probabilities being carried out on threats that are known to have little, or no, impact?

- Is a consistent approach being taken to assessing potential impact, probability and possible action?

- Is there a good understanding of the relationship between the potential impact and the probability of the risk occurring?

- Is the risk information required communicated effectively to support the necessary decision making process, in a timely, clear and cost effective manner?

- Is there a clear understanding of the difference between a problem/issue management process and the risk process, and is there a suitable means of transferring from one to the other?

- Is there an understanding and commitment as to what level of risk is acceptable for a project, and the ability to communicate this? Does this reflect the potential for accruing benefits?

- Are the appropriate skills required to carry out the analysis available?

- Are risks being understated or overstated when assessed or evaluated, whether for commercial, political or individual reasons?

- Is there adequate commitment at all levels to the process of analysing and evaluating the threats? How was this established and are mechanisms in place to maintain commitment?

- Is the process of analysing and evaluating the threats sufficiently flexible to be able to respond to rapid change? For example, e-commerce developments increasingly require IT developers or other parts of the business, such as business relationship management, human resources, facilities etc., to gear up to deliver a solution to the 'market' within abnormally tight timescales.

- Is there a demonstrable correlation between the planned risk management activities (including assessment) and the risk to the level of exposure that it could engender?

- Is a consistent approach being taken regarding the identification and prioritisation of the risks in the risk management process and in any associated issue management process?

3.6   Response to risk

Decisions need to be taken on how to respond to the specific risk by taking action to improve the situation. Possible responses to risk may include :

- transferring some aspects of the risk – perhaps by paying a third party to take it on (a major feature of the Private Finance Initiative); note that business and reputational risk cannot be transferred. Insurance is another method to use to transfer some elements of risk

- tolerating the risk – perhaps because nothing can be done at a reasonable cost to mitigate it, although, ideally, the risk should be monitored to ensure it remains tolerable

- treating the risk – take action to control it in some way by applying containment or contingent actions. Within this categorisation:

  - containment actions are those which lessen the likelihood of the risk or the consequences and are applied before the risk materialises

  - contingent actions are those which are put into action after the risk has happened. Here the focus is on reducing the impact of the risk. These actions can be preplanned so that people know what to do in advance

- terminating the risk – by doing things differently and thus removing the risk, where it is feasible to do so.

Responses should be proportional to the risk. Apart from the most extreme circumstances it is usually enough to have controls that give a reasonable assurance of confining likely loss to acceptable limits for the organisation, programme, project, or operational environment. Every response has an associated cost, if the risk should materialise; the response must offer value for money in relation to the risk that it is controlling. In general, the purpose of the control is to contain risk rather than remove it.

The risk response process should involve identifying and evaluating a significant range of options for treating risks, and preparing and implementing risk management plans. There are different approaches for reducing risks, as shown in Table 3 below, each of which will affect the organisation's level of confidence in achieving its objectives.

Table 3: Approaches for the reduction of risk (based on BS6079)

Measures to reduce risk	
Eliminating or avoiding (typically directive or preventive)	Changing or abandoning goals or objectives specifically associated with the risk in question, or choosing alternative approaches or processes that remove the risk
Risk sharing (typically directive)	Sharing risks in part or full with another stakeholder who could be involved solely to facilitate risk treatment, e.g. an insurer
Reducing the possibility (typically preventive or directive)	Changing approach identifying causal links between threat and impact, or sources of threat and intervening to mitigate occurrence, acting to reduce the threat
Reducing the consequences (typically detective or corrective)	Developing contingency plans for responding to the threat if it occurs, even if other steps have been taken to minimise the risk. Insurance cover may be used to retrieve the situation

Each approach may combine the different categories of control as described in Table 4 below.

Table 4: Categories of control

Category of control	Description
Directive	Designed to ensure that the particular outcome is achieved. Typically associated with health and safety. Wearing protective clothing during performance of dangerous tasks, or insisting on staff being trained before starting a project. Also includes risk sharing (e.g. insurance).
Preventive	Designed to limit the possibility of an undesirable outcome being realised. The majority of controls fall into this category. Separation of duty to prevent fraud is an example.
Detective	Designed to identify occasions of undesirable outcomes having been realised. Their effect is after the event, so they are only appropriate where it is possible to accept the loss or damage incurred. Examples include stock or asset checks, reconciliations and post-implementation reviews that identify lessons learned from projects for future application.
Corrective	Designed to correct undesirable outcomes that have been realised. They provide a route of recourse to achieve some recovery against loss or damage. An example of this would be design of contract terms to allow recovery of overpayment. Insurance can be regarded as a form of corrective control.

Responding to risks involves balancing the ability to complete the activity and realising the benefits that you were hoping to achieve. Sometimes it is appropriate to place the activity 'at risk' because this will open up greater opportunities for the future. But the full reasoning behind such a decision must be clearly articulated and documented so that there is an audit trail of the decision. This will then show that the decision was well based at that time should circumstances change in the future. Issues to consider, and document, include:

- What are the benefits of the possible containment or contingent actions?

- Can we ignore this risk (at this time)?

- Is further analysis required to gain a clear picture of the appropriate actions to take?

You should simplify the overall picture so that it is possible to see which actions will be of benefit (this may require risks to be grouped in relation to potential reduction strategies, as one action may well affect the potential of several risks).

You should also assess the relative severity of risk and prioritise the actions to be taken. Where significant uncertainty still exists it may be necessary to undertake further analysis before finalising plans. Of particular concern is the need to identify:

- resource requirements and costs (as contained in a plan to address the risk)

- triggers (or prompts) which would instigate action, including assignment of ownership of risk action (against either threat or risk, or reduce opportunity).

Process to identify suitable responses to risk

The process objective is:

- for each major risk – threats and opportunities – identify several potential responses

The process activities are:

- Identify a range of practical responses to each significant risk on the Risk Register.

- Investigate if the responses themselves create an opportunity or pose a threat to other areas of activity and identify these links.

- Sort the risks into priority order.

- Cross reference risks to the responses.

- Update the Risk Register with this information.

Practical pointers for this process are listed below.

- Identifying and quantifying risks, in particular technical risks, needs to be done as early as possible to ensure that the widest set of responses is available for consideration.

- If a risk has a high impact then it is possible that some action should be identified to address it. If probability is not significant then the action will be contingent. Where probability is high and impact is low it is likely that the risk will be accepted without planning any direct response.

Checklist: risk response

- Have the treatment measures recommended been assessed in terms of:
  - costs compared with the anticipated benefits of treating the risk?
  - the range of responses available?
  - the effectiveness in containing the risk or enhancing the opportunity?
- Do the risks have an adequate description that can be fully understood?
- Have the risks been assessed and prioritised to see which needs tackling first?
- Has the subsequent required treatment been set and agreed?
- Has there been a clear allocation of responsibilities and ownership for actions, decisions, etc. and the required timescales for completion and review?
- Has the information required for communicating been identified, i.e, to whom, where and when and how?
- Is there a mechanism in place for monitoring and reporting on the effectiveness of the actions being undertaken?
- Has adequate contingency been planned to maintain the risk exposure within the designated risk tolerance level?

3.7 Implementing risk responses

Your responses to risk should ensure that risk exposure is within toleration and that the actions are within budget. Some risk responses may reduce the overall potential benefits and this loss must be taken into account when deciding on which action to take.

Once selected, responses must have appropriate plans agreed which may affect project or programme plans, or contingency plans (see Annex F for more on business continuity management).

Process to implement risk responses

The process objectives are to:

- select the most appropriate response to all significant risks
- finalise associated plans and gain approval
- ensure appropriate information on risk is communicated to appropriate management
- implement plans.

The process activities are:

- Analyse the overall exposure to risk against the 'risk tolerance level'.
- Select the most appropriate set of responses.
- Analyse whether these responses produce additional unintended consequences – if so, further planning is required.
- Identify owners for risk threats and responses.

- Finalise the plans for activity and any subsequent contingency/business continuity plans.

- Update Risk Register and ensure managers receive appropriate information.

- Gain approval to the plans and risk ownership allocation.

- Allocate resources to the plans and/or assign responsibilities for risk.

Practical pointers for this process are listed below.

- Owners may be identified to be responsible for ensuring risk actions are carried out effectively. The risk owners need to have suitable authority to be given this responsibility.

- Some risk responses may address more than one threat.

- Where appropriate, plans to address risk must be incorporated into 'normal activity plans' (such as the project or programme plan) rather than maintaining separate risk management plans.

- Plans must also ensure that approaches to manage the risk can be measured for their effectiveness. Identifying metrics and ensuring these can be measured will form part of the monitoring and approval process.

3.8   Monitoring responses

When risk response actions have been implemented, the risks still need to be monitored. One of the most common approaches is the use of Risk Registers (often called Risk Logs). The advantage is that all the information on each risk is maintained in one place in the Risk Register, so that a complete picture of risk exposure can be built up. Figure 5 below shows a basic set of contents, which can be tailored as required.

Risk ID No.	Raised By And Date	Description of the Risk (Source or threat)	Impact VL, L, M, H, VH			Prob. VL, L, M, H, VH	Proximity	Action	Target Date	Owner
			Time	Cost	Quality					
1			L	L	M	VL				
2			H	H	M	M				
3			H	L	VH	H				

Figure 5: Extract from a typical Risk Register

The Risk Register may have an associated 'Summary Risk Profile'. This provides a quick view of the overall exposure to risk as documented in the Risk Register (see Chapter 8 for more information on risk profiles).

3.9   Assurance and review

There must be mechanisms in place for monitoring and reporting effectiveness in managing risk. A reporting system should be in place to enable regular, upward reporting on the work done to keep risk and control procedures up to date and in line with business need. This reporting system should be owned by, and ultimately report to, the Accounting Officer.

There are two levels of assurance: ensuring risk is controlled in particular situations and assessing whether risk management processes are adopted adequately (see Figure 4).

For the first level of assurance, you should continually monitor the situation in relation to those risks identified and actions planned. You should also check whether new risks are pending; existing risks may well reduce over time. You will need to revisit plans, plot progress, look for trigger events actually occurring, and watch for changes in circumstance. When changes occur, initiate additional identification and assessment so that replanning can be undertaken where appropriate.

The second level of assurance concerns how well the risk management processes are adopted, rather than how well individual risks are managed. Some parts of the organisation may be more advanced in adopting management of risk and they should assist other areas to create a common level.

Process to gain assurances about effectiveness

The process objectives are:

- to monitor risk responses and assess their effectiveness

- to assess that the activity remains within the risk tolerance level.

The process activities are:

- Gather information about risk responses.

- Reassess the exposure to risk and update the Risk Register.

- Re-evaluate activity.

- Check that risks are still within agreed tolerances and make this information available for external audit/review.

Practical pointers for this process are listed below.

- Responses must be clearly defined so that it is possible to assess their effectiveness. If appropriate measurements cannot be collected the analysis here will be limited

- The emphasis here is on how well risks themselves are identified and managed (not how effective the management of risk processes are being applied).

Checklist: monitoring and control mechanisms

- Has appropriate ownership of the status reporting mechanism been achieved (that is, how it will be used, when and by whom as the owners and expeditors of that process)?

- Has the organisation put in place mechanisms to monitor the adequacy of processes required to ensure that cultural, political and personal pressures do not hinder truthful representation of status of high-profile risks?

- Is there confidence in the accuracy of reporting?

- Is the level of commitment to the reporting process adequate or is there a lack of commitment?

- When assessing and reporting effectiveness are the statements made factual rather than speculative?

3.10   Continuing to improve

Your organisation should aim for continuous improvement in its management of risk. The effectiveness of your organisation in deploying the processes described in this chapter can be assessed using the checklists provided:

- a high-level checklist to indicate whether the existing process is as effective as perceived (Annex B)

- a series of brief checklists for self-assessments or 'healthchecks' against the various components of risk management (see earlier sections in this chapter, repeated in Annex B).

Process to embed and review management of risk

The process objective is:

- to produce a report on how well the management of risk processes and framework are embedded into everyday management activities.

The process activities are:

- Assess application of the management of risk processes (Annex B provides checklists).

- Review effectiveness of the application and the maturity of the organisation.

- Identify areas for change/improvement.

- Produce a report on effectiveness and pass to management.

Practical pointers for this process are listed below.

- The review of practical application of management of risk will normally be done annually as part of the support for corporate governance.

- The report on effectiveness will include areas for improvement and so may include initial plans for how these might be achieved.

4

CHAPTER 4: MANAGING RISK AT THE STRATEGIC LEVEL

Management of risk at the strategic (or corporate) level is concerned with setting strategic direction and balancing potential opportunity against the costs and risks. It is normally at this level that the widest context of the business is reviewed – its financial, legislative, political, social, competitive and cultural environments.

Corporate/departmental and programme objectives and goals are being set, and management of risk must be carried out in line with these. For example, an organisation may be thinking about innovative ways of delivering business services that involve new technologies. Options for exploiting opportunities for improved performance need to be assessed against the risks associated with relatively unproven technologies and/or collaboration with private sector partners.

Since much of the risk identification and analysis conducted at the strategic level will be intuitive in nature, there is a need for a formal approach to the management of risk to ensure that the decisions made are of the highest quality possible. In addition, if a formal analysis approach is followed, the information on risks identified at this level can be passed down the organisation for further analysis and resolution.

4.1   Types of risk

At the strategic level the concerns are about where the organisation wants to go, how to get there and how to ensure survival. Risks are typically concerned with commercial, financial, directional, environmental, cultural, acquisition, political and quality issues. The materialisation of major risks at this level is likely to stop the organisation functioning.

Programme, project and operational risks should be escalated to this level against set criteria where they exceed agreed tolerances – such as if there is an unacceptable exposure to risk, if they fall outside certain limits or if they could affect strategic objectives.

4.2   Where to apply risk management

Without a clear view of the strategic objectives and goals, risk analysis and management may be inappropriately applied at all levels of the organisation. Commitments to corporate governance are made at this level. Decisions are taken on future strategy and changes to commercial arrangements, which could involve issues relating to the business, technical environment, people, accommodation or the start of a new acquisition lifecycle. Considerations about commercial arrangements include setting the overall approach to working with partners and use of the Private Finance Initiative (PFI).

Senior managers therefore need to understand the risks associated with their decisions and actions; there must be the involvement of the management board, especially the Accounting Officer.

4.3   When to do it

At the strategic level, risk management activities should be triggered when:

- identifying, reviewing, agreeing and setting corporate/departmental objectives and goals, to be done on a periodic basis to ensure influences and risk factors have not changed; at this level at least annually

- assessing and choosing options for implementation of strategic initiatives

- formulating, submitting or reviewing feasibility studies/business cases to support future strategies

- testing the underlying assumptions within the business case or proposed strategies

- formally instigating, approving or reviewing programmes, projects and operational activities (including their objectives, goals and performance)

- there is any indication that changes in external factors, such as political, social, economic, regulatory, commercial or financial issues could affect the strategy, mission, objectives and goals

- there have been changes in, or potential changes are identified to, stakeholder involvement

- an unforeseen event has occurred that could have an impact on the corporate objectives, such as a change in regulations

- making key acquisition decisions, for example, at the start of a new acquisition lifecycle.

4.4   Who is involved

Table 5 summarises the roles and responsibilities of those involved in management of risk at the strategic level.

Table 5: Who is involved

Who should own and apply the risk process	Responsibilities
Management Board	Ownership of the overall management of risk framework and process
Accounting Officers, Directors, Steering Groups, Stakeholders, SROs	Establishing policy on risk and signing off risk strategy, including willingness to take on risk and risk tolerance levels
Business consultants, technical strategists	Application of risk process to business changes, such as in strategy, establishment of new programmes
Risk Committee, Audit Committee	Ensuring compliance with corporate/departmental guidance on internal control

Who should own and apply the risk process	Responsibilities
Legal, financial, procurement advisors	Managing legal, commercial, market related risks. Ensure risks are reported to appropriate levels and responses made
Specialist advisors, such as security/business continuity management	Approval of budgets to be allocated to the management of risk
Gateway Teams	Assessment at Gate, in particular Gate 0, may be required at this level

4.5   Strategic level policy for management of risk

Strategic level policy should be in the form of a high-level statement showing how management of risk will be handled throughout the organisation with guidance on roles, responsibilities, processes and procedures.

Composition of the policy

- Management of risk process (as in Figure 4) and any adaptations to be made for application to the organisation

- Statement of benefits to be achieved through management of risk in general and specifically at the strategic level

- The level and nature of risk which is acceptable (this may be supported by identifying authorised business activities and programmes)

- Responsibility for management of risk activities – e.g. owner of this product

- Owner of the management of risk process

- Owner/s for major programmes

- Roles and responsibilities of stakeholders and the relative significance of time, cost, benefits, business/political risk and quality to these people to include responsibility for monitoring application of management of risk

- Identify mechanisms for monitoring the successful application of this policy and associated reporting mechanisms

- Identify internal (and, if appropriate, external control mechanisms to be put in place to independently assess policy implementation)

- Identify generic rules for allocating severity to risks (probability and impact)

- Clarify rules for escalation of risk information at least from programme and operational levels to strategic level

- Identify how inter-programme dependencies will be identified and managed, also those relating to initiatives (new or changing)

- Identify standard documentation forms/standards and supporting facilities and tools. For example, use the contents of Risk Register, Summary Risk Profile and stakeholder maps

- Relationship with specific policies and guidelines (if available, especially those related to acquisition, safety, security and business continuity).

5

CHAPTER 5: MANAGING RISK AT THE PROGRAMME LEVEL

Managers at the programme, or middle, management level have the most difficult task of all. They are responsible for transforming high-level strategy into politically acceptable solutions. These managers are typically responsible for a number of projects. The risk and opportunity trade-offs involved become even more complex as projects compete with one another for resources. The managers are primarily responsible for identifying and detailing solutions to conflicts associated with the implementation of strategic plans over which they have little influence. In addition, programme level managers have to act as 'firefighters' – responsible for keeping specific project crises from getting out of control and affecting the strategic objectives of the organisation.

To help deal with concerns at this level, programme managers will have the strategic-level risk policy that sets down processes, procedures and roles and responsibilities for use across the organisation.

5.1   Areas of risk

The risks associated with programmes to achieve major business change are complex and interrelated. Changes in one aspect could affect all the others – the business environment, the internal organisation, its people and technology (see Figure 6).

Breaking down a programme

It may be necessary to split the programme into a collection of projects in order to achieve the required business benefits.

Business benefit

Major products (or components) are identified and delivered through a project. The delivery of each component can then be prioritised to gain maximum benefit at the earliest possible occasion. In some instances it may be beneficial to deliver a component that is seen as low-value, but also low-risk, in order to familiarise the organisation and stakeholders with the delivery issues. The higher risk aspects can be tackled once some experience has been gained.

Culture

A primary consideration is the ability of the culture of the organisation to accommodate change and the ability of the organisation's leadership to drive the change through.

Breaking the change into smaller parts (possibly projects) allows the culture of the organisation to become familiar gradually with change, which can then allow more radical moves in the future.

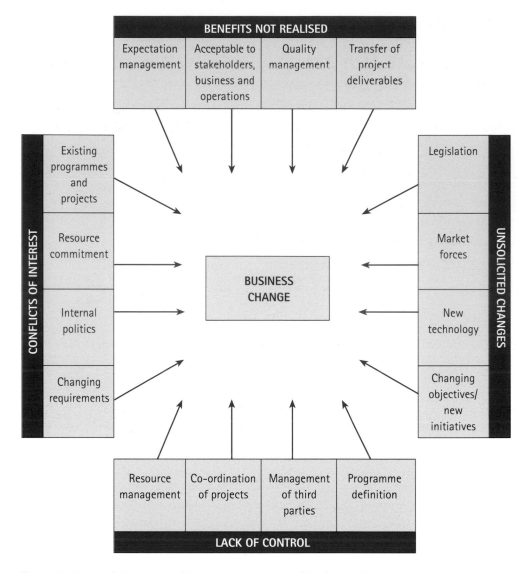

Figure 6: Areas of risk to consider in programmes of business change

As part of the cultural assessment, you need to consider the amount of change the organisation is undergoing concurrently – the more changes that are imposed, the greater the risk of failure.

Acquisition

Acquiring the components needs to be considered early, as the procurement/contractual process can take a considerable time, particularly if protracted international procedures are involved.

Change control

Each component should be delivered to specification. Any prospective changes must be identified and considered in terms of benefits and impact on the programme as a whole, not just the individual project or component.

5.2   Types of risk

Typical risks at the programme level are associated with acquisition, funding, organisational and cultural issues, projects, security, safety, quality and business continuity.

Project and operational risks should be escalated to this level against set criteria where they exceed agreed tolerances, such as an unacceptable exposure to risk, if they fall outside certain limits or if they could affect programme objectives.

Before initiating any programme or major project, the organisation should make a realistic assessment of its readiness to cope with complex change. These questions provide an indicator of the issues that should be probed:

- is there a clear direction set out in the business strategy?

- is there ongoing alignment to the strategy?

- are roles and responsibilities understood and accepted by top management?

- is there access to the right skills and capabilities?

- is there learning from experience in managing change?

- is there a framework for managing risk?

If these preconditions for success are not met, any programme or project is at high risk. These questions should be revisited at each significant decision point in a programme or major project.

5.3   Where to apply risk management

Risk management at this level should be applied where:

- the information about risk can influence the programme most effectively, such as where critical decisions are to be taken

- decisions being taken at the strategic level require programme risk information

- programme objectives are, or will be, influenced by changes to strategic objectives and vice versa

- the business case for the programme or associated projects is being revised or reviewed

- there is a requirement for a Gateway Review.

The risk analyses will need to be conducted at two levels:

- considering projects as individual elements of strategy implementation

- considering all the projects that make up a programme as representing a single entity.

Where appropriate, decisions about risk at this level form an important part of the business case.

5.4   When to do it

At the programme level risk management should be triggered when:

- reviewing and reporting programme status with regard to corporate and programme objectives (known as Programme Benefit Reviews)

- providing formal approval for, or reviewing projects against, programme and project objectives, goals, business case and performance

- endeavouring to engage stakeholders in the programme

- conducting programme planning or rescheduling

- key projects show symptoms of failing, or have failed to meet their objectives

- starting a new acquisition lifecycle of a programme

- preparing for Gateway Reviews

- significant changes are proposed, planned or have occurred at any of the other levels – that is, strategy, project, operations or within the external environment

- they are an integral part of the programme/project management process, such as PRINCE2 – for example, when the Risk Register is updated and reviewed.

5.5   Who is involved

Table 6 summarises the roles and responsibilities involved in risk management at the programme level.

Table 6: Who is involved

Who should own and apply the risk process	Responsibilities
SROs	Approve funding for programme and project risk management plans
Programme Director	Balancing an acceptable level of programme risk against business opportunity and deciding level of acceptability of individual risks
Sponsors/Sponsoring Group	Establishing and assuring the effectiveness of the risk process to be used at project level, including guidance on tools and techniques to be used
Accounting Officers	Categorising and prioritising risks across the various projects, including setting or validating tolerance levels for risk at project level
Programme Director and Managers	Ensuring that the design process, technical change control and quality assurance address risk
Programme Delivery Manager	Approve and sign off project risk management plans and monitor status and effectiveness of process and plans

Who should own and apply the risk process	Responsibilities
Programme Support Office	Escalation of risks to business executive, Accounting Officers, stakeholders and appropriate management boards
Programme risk specialists, e.g. security Business Change Managers Procurement Managers Contract managers Legal, regulatory advisors Business Continuity Managers	Check feasibility of technical risks through appropriate authority Advise and provide guidance to projects on project risk within the context of the programme and relevant strategy
Gateway Review teams	Involvement in Gate reviews, especially Gates 0, 1 and 5

5.6   Programme level policy for management of risk

Programme level policy should be in the form of a high-level statement showing how management of risk will be handled during the lifetime of the programme.

Composition of the policy

- Refer to strategic-level management of risk policy identifying those elements that apply and any areas that deviate from that policy.

- Any specific benefits associated with this policy.

- Identify nature and level of risk acceptable within the programme and associated projects.

- Identify scale to be used to assess severity of risk (probability and impact).

- Clarify rules of escalation from projects to the programme.

- Identify responsibility for management of risk activities: owner of this policy (e.g. senior manager or Programme Director).

- Owner of the programme (e.g. senior manager or Programme Director).

- Owners for individual projects – Project SRO/Sponsor/project executive.

- Identify roles and responsibilities of stakeholders with regard to risk.

- Identify mechanisms for monitoring successful applications of this policy within the programme and its projects.

- Identify how inter-project dependencies will be identified and managed.

- Confirm documentation standards, forms and supporting facilities, tools and techniques.

- Relationship to associated initiatives and programmes, policies and guidelines.

6

CHAPTER 6: MANAGING RISKS AT THE PROJECT LEVEL

Risk management at the project level focuses on keeping unwanted outcomes to the minimum. Decisions about risk management at this level form an important part of the business case; where providers and/or partners are involved you must gain a shared view of the risks and how they will be managed. As part of the tool kit for dealing with issues at this level, project managers will have the programme risk policy or the strategic-level risk policy to give overall guidance on management of risk aspects.

Optimising risks, costs and benefits starts with the early anticipation of problems through the identification of risks. Control can be established from the outset through good programme and project organisation, processes and communications. It is essential to allocate responsibility realistically; this increases accountability and builds a greater confidence in the overall success of the project. Benefits can be realised through a common understanding of what is achievable and a commitment to achieve it.

6.1 Breaking down a project

A major project involving business change is usually broken down into manageable chunks of work (components). Each piece of work will develop a product (outcome or deliverable) to support the required business change.

Factors to consider when breaking it down include setting limits on:

- maximum time to develop the component/product (preferably no more than 18 months for development of an individual component)

- cost/resource effort (maximum expenditure)

- scope of business functionality to be supported. It may be useful to develop a product to support part of the overall requirement and get this in use early, before expanding, so the product supports the full requirement.

An important part of any project is the implementation stage. The organisation needs to be prepared with the necessary infrastructure and trained personnel in place to accept the final product.

Following development, it can be useful to have a pilot stage to monitor usage of the component in a controlled environment for a limited period of time, before rolling out the whole organisation.

It is also important to know what has been released in this way. Thus all products should be subjected to configuration management to control the products. With effective configuration management in place, multiple changes can be made almost simultaneously.

Testing should be related directly to development, so that each product has associated test (acceptance) activity to ensure they meet requirements. This may involve testing individual products or sets of products before they are used in a working business environment.

6.2   Types of risk

Risks at the project level typically include personal, technical, cost, schedule, resource, operational support, quality and supplier failure issues. Operational issues will also need to be considered where they are relevant to the outcomes of the project. Strategic and programme related risks should be communicated to this level where they could affect project objectives.

Risks relating to individual projects should be communicated to other projects and operations where appropriate.

Risks at this level could occur in the following three areas:

- **scope**: is the scope of the project well defined and related to business objectives?

- **resources**: does the project team have the skills, competencies and support to deliver?

- **process**: are there well defined processes for managing the project, risk etc?

If these risks are not managed, the project will be out of control.

6.3   Where to apply risk management

Risk management at the project level should be applied where:

- project objectives and goal are being assessed

- project initiation is being carried as part of the project lifecycle and when using the Project Profile Model (see Chapter 8).

At this level, the primary concern is to carry out action guidelines developed at the programme level. Depending on how well the risks are analysed and managed at the corporate and programme levels, the task of managing risk at the project level is either minimal or intensive. If there is strong commitment to the management of risk process at high levels of the organisation, most of the management of risk at project level will already be defined and documented; it simply needs to be checked and then followed.

To initiate a project some basic information is required, including terms of reference, boundary of scope, initial plans and the appropriate details of risk analysis completed at the higher levels.

The risk analysis techniques are analytical in nature and focus on determining the impact of underperformance risks. But one of the major threats to a project is lack of understanding of the scope of the project. This area needs to be carefully considered, particularly project definition and control of change. Where the project carries a lot of uncertainty, as when using novel approaches or technology, the risk analysis is less precise at first. In this situation, the need for re-evaluation of risk is greater. The risk analysis techniques may also be more subjective than those used in other projects.

6.4   When to do it

At the project level, risk management should be triggered when:

- there is a change in the project lifecycle, such as each major phase, stage and decision point of the project and as part of the project planning process

- major acquisitions are being made as part of the project

- reassessing project benefits and the business case

- preparing to hand over from a development environment to operations

- any significant changes are notified to the project, such as reorganisation, change of supplier, unforeseen changes to other interdependencies such as connected projects or programmes

- revisiting the cost-benefit and risk case behind the project or programme

- preparing for Gateway Reviews.

6.5   Who is involved

Table 7 summarises the roles and responsibilities involved in risk management at the project level.

Table 7: Who is involved

Who should own and apply the risk process	Responsibilities
Project Boards SROs Project Sponsors	Balancing an acceptable level of project risk against programme and project objectives and business opportunity
Project managers Project support office Project risk specialists	Implementing the management of risk process to be used at project level Ensuring interdependency related risks are reported and addressed
Project Delivery Managers Operations Managers	Escalation of risks to programme level and operations where required and responding to risks notified to the project
Project Work Groups/teams Business Continuity/ Security Managers	Allocation of project resources to support the risk process
Project auditors	Approval of funding for project risk related activities
Gateway Review teams	Involvement in reviews at Gates

6.6   Project level policy for management of risk

Project level policy should be in the form of a high-level statement showing how management of risk will be handled during the lifetime of the project.

Composition of the policy

- Reference to programme management of risk policy (or if not applicable, to strategic-level management of risk policy), to identify the overall application of the process – roles, responsibility and escalation rules

- Any additional benefits associated with adoption of management of risk on this project

- Identify nature and level of risk acceptable within the project (risk tolerance level)

- Clarify scales to be used to assess severity of risk (impact and probability)

- Confirm rules for escalating risk information/decision making

- Identify responsibilities for management of risk activities: owners of this product and the management of risk process owner of the project

- Identify roles and responsibilities of stakeholders with regard to risk

- Confirm how monitoring mechanisms will be implemented and reported on

- Confirm facilities, tools, techniques and documentation standards to be used

- Relationship to associated programme, projects, policies and standards

- Relationship to third parties through contracts and how associated risks need to be managed.

7

CHAPTER 7: MANAGING RISK AT THE OPERATIONAL LEVEL

Risk management at the operational level is primarily concerned with continuity of business services. You may have suppliers who are carrying out risk management relating to your services, but there should be a shared understanding and agreement on the risks and who will manage them.

Management of risk at the operational level of an organisation is similar to that at the project level. While project risk efforts are more concerned with implementation efforts, the operational manager is aiming to deliver a product or service, day after day and week after week.

The manager must focus on the risk of not being able to provide the product or service to an adequate level of quality. Service level agreements may apply defining the required timing, (response) cost, quality and level of security (see Annex G for a discussion of the relationship between security and risk).

Risk analysis techniques for assessing and managing operational risks may range from simple audits to ensure that performance is, and is expected to remain, adequate, to full analyses to discover the risks involved in an upgrade. A major concern is the adaptability of the operation to cope with sudden change.

7.1 Types of risk

Risks at the operational level typically include personal risks; technical, cost, schedule, resource, operational support, quality, supplier failure and environmental issues; and infrastructure failure. All the higher levels have input to this level; specific concerns include business continuity management, contingency planning, support for business processes and business customer relations.

Major risks could occur during operational service if they are not addressed early on during the acquisition/procurement process:

- **scope**: ongoing risks relating to the scope of the contract, including planned and unplanned change
- **resources**: ongoing risks relating to the skills and competencies of the contract management team
- **process**: ongoing risks relating to processes such as service management.

If these risks are not managed, the service will not achieve its business benefits and costs will escalate.

7.2   Where to apply risk management

Risk management at the operational level should be applied where:

- delivery of projects will impose either a significant change, or a potential risk, to the operational environment – for example, the deliverables are of inadequate quality

- timescales for delivery put pressure upon the operational environment. Serious conflict can result if the objectives of different project drivers and owners are not synchronised. Operational people need to allow for and schedule in the impact of such changes

- changes in the operational environment could significantly undermine the project, programme and strategic objectives if the risks are not understood and communicated

- there is a requirement to identify the critical business process and technology

- changes are required to a contract with a key supplier or service provider, or supplier performance is being assessed

- there is a need to build commitment to change (cultural or otherwise)

- there is a need for internal control from a corporate governance perspective – for example, an IT project that delivers a system with poor information security controls or no business continuity strategy could create a corporate governance problem

- there are regulatory and legal constraints, such as health and safety, data protection and information.

7.3   When to do it

At the operational level, risk management should be triggered when:

- considering undertaking significant commitments on behalf of the organisation – for example, changing providers or starting new contracts, or major new acquisitions

- establishing a new operational process or considering any significant change to the existing operational environment – for example, relocation, downsizing, significant maintenance shutdowns

- major investment decisions are being made

- identifying future human resource requirements for operational staff

- there is a perceived unexpected threat to the operational environment, e.g. environmental issues, demonstrations

- anything unforeseen that happens and threatens 'business as usual'.

7.4   Who is involved

Table 8 summarises the roles and responsibilities involved in risk management at the operational level.

Table 8: Who is involved

Who should own and apply the risk process	Responsibilities
IT Directors/Managers Business managers Operations managers	Balancing an acceptable level of operational risk against programme and project objectives and business opportunity
Finance Director/Accounting Officer	Implementing the risk process to be used at the operational level
Information Security Manager Operational support staff	Ensuring interdependency related risks at the operational level are reported and addressed
Business Continuity Manager	Escalation of risks to strategic, programme and project level where required
Health and Safety Officer	Allocation of resources to support the risk process
Facilities Manager Human Resource Managers Legal and regulatory officers Practitioners supporting the process, e.g. information security, business continuity, software engineers Auditors	Approval of funding for operational risk activities
Gateway Review teams	Involvement in reviews at Gates 4 and 5

7.5   Operational level policy for management of risk

The purpose of a management of risk policy at this level is to define how risks will be managed during the lifetime of the service. In particular it is used to show close links to security, business continuity and contingency plans.

Composition of the policy

Show how the strategic-level management of risk policy is adopted and also ensure any risk policies of related programme and project are reflected appropriately.

● Show how the strategic-level management of risk policy is adopted and also link to any related risk policies including those for programmes, projects, other operations and suppliers

● Any additional benefits associated with adopting management of risk for operations/services covered

● Confirmation of scope of the policy to be identified (either to a single service or a range of operational activities)

● What type of risks are to be managed

● Level of risk that is acceptable

● Who is responsible for management of risk activities – e.g. owner of this policy

- Owner of management of risk process as applied through this policy (if different from the policy risk owner)

- Owner of individual services encompassed by this policy

- Roles and responsibilities with regard to risk, in particular ensuring contingency, business continuity and security, are covered as part of the support to overall management of risk

- Identify mechanisms for monitoring the successful application of the policy and the associated reporting mechanisms

- Clarify rules for escalating information on risk

- Identify facilities, tools, techniques and documentation standards to be provided

- Cross-references to details of the operations covered.

8

CHAPTER 8: TECHNIQUES

This chapter gives an indication of the range of techniques that can be used to support the management of risk process. It is important to note that experience in managing risk is a more critical factor for success than the choice of tools and techniques.

However, the right support can make it much easier to identify and monitor risks. Gateway Reviews, while not strictly defined as techniques, are helpful in identifying problems that must be addressed, especially in the critical early stages of a project. A Summary Risk Profile, supported by a Risk Register (see Section 8.3), will help you raise the visibility of risk exposure to senior management.

You will find further information on techniques in Annex H.

8.1   Risk identification approaches

This section identifies the major techniques used in this context.

Checklists and promptlists (see Annex C), workshops, questionnaires and brainstorming are widely used to support risk identification. When running workshops, the use of promptlists, questionnaires and interviews to gather information on the threats means the workshop can be used to validate the list of risks and agree their severity, or even propose ways of addressing them.

The output of risk identification should be documented in a consistent way across the organisation, for example, by using a Risk Register (see Section 8.3).

Strategic/corporate level

At this level you will be making business-focused decisions based on options analysis and investment appraisal. It may be appropriate to use the Business Excellence Model to identify how well your organisation is performing, in addition to adopting some of the following techniques:

- NPV (net present value)
- IRR (internal rate of return)
- ROI (Return on Investment)
- cashflow analysis
- currency analysis
- SWOT (strengths, weaknesses, opportunities and threats) analysis
- scenarios
- cost-benefit analysis

- decision trees

- CRAMM for business impact security requirements.

Programme level

At this level your primary focus is the management of interdependencies between the projects that make up the programme and the wider business environment. Techniques include:

- decision trees

- CPA (Critical Path Analysis)

- cost-benefit analysis

- sensitivity analysis

- stakeholder risk analysis

- simulations

- scenarios

- LCC (lifecycle costing analysis).

Project level

At this level you are seeking to avoid the consequences of unwanted outcomes. Techniques to help would include:

- simulations

- LCC

- decision trees

- risk tables

- PERT (Programme Evaluation and Review Technique)

- performance analysis

- reliability analysis

- capability analysis

- Monte Carlo simulation

- influence diagrams

- CRAMM.

Operational level

As with the project level, your main objective is to avoid the consequences of unwanted outcomes. Techniques include:

- simulations

- LCC

- performance analysis

- reliability analysis

- queuing analysis

- algorithm analysis

- capability analysis

- top down analysis

- Hazop (HAZard and OPerability analysis, risk registers and databases)

- CRAMM.

8.2   Risk management approaches

Techniques here relate to good general management and need to cover:

- assignment of responsibility (in particular risk ownership)

- planning and scheduling of resources; monitoring progress against plan

- risk status reporting (to different people as appropriate)

- benchmarking.

Other useful techniques will relate to development/production of the correct product, including Critical Path Analysis; prototyping; requirements management; supplier/contract management; configuration management; quality control/management.

All levels

Table 9 provides additional information on use of some of the most commonly adopted techniques.

8.3   Documentation techniques

Models are useful for comparing the results of evaluation of individual risks at various levels. Spreadsheets are often used to develop an overview of a Summary Risk Profile. However, it is important to note that the building of a risk model, like the categorisation of risk, involves subjective judgement both in the input to the model and in the interpretation of results.

Experience with such models shows that you must be prepared to tailor them to your organisation's circumstances; models acquired from external sources such as this guidance can only offer a starting point for developing the 'right' model for the particular organisation.

Table 9: Relative use of techniques

Method	1. Expected monetary value [1]	2. Visual interactive simulation [2]	3. Monte Carlo	4. Decision trees	5. Grids [3]	6. Critical path analysis
Circumstances used	Expected profit or loss	To identify optimal solutions	Financial modelling: Investigating sensitivity of risk models	Decision analysis	Relates hazards and potential victims to identify priority actions	Optimise complex activities
Type of data needed	Probability of event and risk event values	Probability of timings and distributions	Interest rates etc.	Probability of event and expected values	None	Time and cost data
Skills needed	Mathematical and statistical	Computer package and statistics	Spreadsheet Monte Carlo model	Statistics	–	–
Examples of use	Budget decisions	Scheduling of resources	Cash flow predictions	Choice of investment	Stakeholder risk analysis	Mapping of critical inter-dependencies
Advantages	Simple and easy to use	Powerful. Detailed. Robust	Stochastic. Realistic	Single number answer	Identifies risks (threats)	Overview of whole project
Disadvantages	Too basic. Probabilities have to be known and investigated	Could be used for wrong purpose	Programming knowledge needed	May over-simplify	Does not reflect probability of risks occurring	Input to CBA could be wrong

Notes
1   For example, NPV
2   For example, simulations, scenarios, performance analysis
3   For example, risk maps, stakeholder risk analysis.

Risk Register

The purpose of a risk register is to maintain information on all the identified risks relating to a specific plan (business, project, etc.), contract or piece of work.

There must be sufficient information to make it worthwhile collating the information, but each organisation will need to decide its own content requirements for each entry. Table 10 shows some typical entries in a Risk Register:

Table 10: Typical entries in a Risk Register

Risk identifier	unique identifier in relation to the activity to which the risk register relates
Risk type	identification of the category of risk (see Annex C)
Risk owner	individual or role that is in a position to exercise some control over this risk
Raised by; person and date	if necessary this person may be asked to clarify why they think a risk exists; the date forms part of the audit trail – by knowing when the risk was identified it is possible to assess the suitability of the actions proposed
Description of risk	brief description so that the analysis can be undertaken
Impact	may be looked at in terms of time, cost and quality. This shows the degree to which the activity will be affected should this risk actually materialise. If consolidating onto a Summary Risk Profile there needs to be a single overall category for impact. Note quality covers aspects of requirement and performance and the nature of this should be clearly stated
Probability	assessment of how likely this risk is to happen – the proposed Summary Risk Profile has five degrees for this (very low, low, medium, high, very high)
Proximity	reflects the timing of the threat of the risk. Is its threat strongest at a particular point in time? Does the threat disappear sometime in the future? Or does its probability or impact change over time?
Possible actions	what might you do to reduce/mitigate the risk? Each option will have associated benefits and costs – these should be included here but may be documented elsewhere if deemed appropriate
Chosen action	action that will be instigated against this risk
Target date or trigger	timing by which action needs to be started (or completed) based on what it is and how it will address the risk – e.g. contingency actions will identify the trigger that would warrant the plan being invoked. Other actions may need to be undertaken at a specific point in time.
Action Owner/ custodian	some actions may not be within the remit of the risk owner to control explicitly; in that situation there should be a nominated owner of the action who will need to keep the risk owner apprised of the situation
Closure date	is there a point in the future when this risk/action is no longer a threat and so this entry can be closed? (It may be archived but should not be lost as the details may be audited at a later date)
X-refs – activity/plan	identify the activity or plan that this risk relates to if that is not already implicit with the details above – for example, for a project the analysed risk will relate to a specific version of a plan; that version should be identified
X-refs – risks	addressing this risk may affect other risks – either because the planned action reduces their severity or by addressing this risk others may be increased – but the overall effect is beneficial. Such linkages should be identified here

Once an organisation is accustomed to analysing risk it may also use status flags. The risk register would then be enhanced with two additional fields. Status can be identified in terms of red/amber/green (or RAG status) flags that help to monitor how effectively risks are being controlled (see Table 11). Two commonly used terms are:

- measure-of-risk RAG status, which reflects the level of exposure that the risk represents to the project. If green it can be accepted in its current form

- action RAG status, which reflects the effectiveness of the action applied to the risk. The action RAG should never show a worse status than the 'measure of risk'. The exception would be if an action to improve the situation regarding one risk makes action on another risk less effective.

Risks are never static; they are always changing. You must monitor not only the effectiveness of the risk assessment process but also risk responses. Any changes should be documented and reflected in the risk register. Where appropriate these should then be reviewed to ensure the most appropriate action is being adopted.

Risk profile models

The Project Profile Model (available at http://www.ogc.gov.uk) has been developed by the Cabinet Office to identify typical problem areas and criticality to the business in terms of scale of a project against central criteria. You must build in your organisation's specific perceptions of risk for the project, such as visibility to the public, in order to assess your organisation's exposure to risk.

A Summary Risk Profile must be used by all central government projects where there is an IT component. This is a simple mechanism to increase visibility of risks; it is a graphical representation of information normally found on an existing risk register. The project manager or risk manager needs to update the risk register on a regular basis and then re-generate the graph, which shows risks in terms of probability and impact with the effects of mitigating action taken into account. The Summary Risk Profile (see Figure 7) shows all key project risks as one picture so that managers can gain an overall impression of the total exposure to risk. It is essential that the graph reflects the time risk exposure – backed up by the information in the Risk Register.

A key feature of this picture is the risk tolerance line, indicated here as a bold line. It shows the overall level of risk that the organisation is prepared to tolerate in a given situation. If exposure to risk is above this line, managers can see that they must take prompt action, such as upward referral of relevant risks.

Setting the risk tolerance line is a task for experienced risk managers; it reflects the organisation's attitudes to risk in general and to a specific set of risks within a project. The parameters of the risk tolerance line should be agreed at the outset between the project manager and senior manager or Project Sponsor and regularly reviewed.

The use of RAG status (mentioned above) can be useful for incorporating the status reporting from risk registers into the risk profiles, and can provide a quick and effective means of monitoring; see Table 11 below.

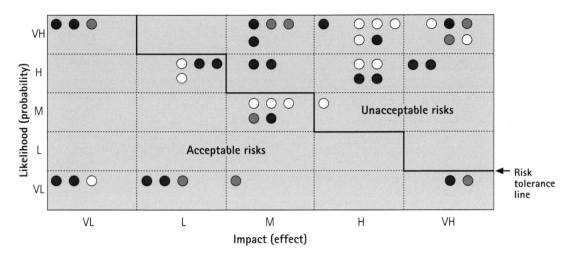

Figure 7: Summary Risk Profile

Table 11: Expanding RAG status for reporting

Colour	Status
None	The risk management action cannot begin until a future specified date, therefore, it is not possible to measure progress
Red	No progress has been made
Amber	Moderate progress being made on risk management action with little/no evidence of the deliverable
Green	Progress is being made, commensurate with the stage of the Project, with appropriate evidence of the deliverable
Blue	Risk management action has been successfully completed and any associated deliverable has been provided

Business Excellence Model

Measuring your organisation's capability can be done in many different ways. One well documented and internationally adopted approach is the Business Excellence Model, also known as the EFQM Excellence Model. This forms a framework for assessment and can be used at overall organisational level, departmental level and/or individual employee level. It consists of nine criteria split between enablers (what we do) and results (what we achieve).

The model provides a scoring framework within each of the nine categories. In the corporate governance area the 'leadership' and 'policy and strategy' aspects are of specific interest. The first checks if people have the authority and responsibility for major aspects of risk management, while the policy assessment examines how well the risk management policies are formulated, reviewed and supported by actions. Specifically it will look for existence of documentation of:

- a framework for management of risk
- security policy (IT, individuals, location)
- business continuity plans.

Thus application of this model will provide an assessment on how well the management of risk is being applied and may identify areas for improvement.

8.4   External review of activities

The Gateway Process is widely used by the private sector to validate the continued viability of projects at key stages in the project management lifecycle, and is now mandatory for all new high-risk projects that involve procurement in central government.

Management of risk is reviewed at each Gate (see Figure 2). The extent and focus of each review is dependent on the purpose of the gate. For further information on Gateway Reviews see http://www.ogc.gov.uk/.

8.5   Applying the risk management processes

Effective use of the risk management process depends on the experience and judgement of practitioners applying the guidance.

The project spiral model is commonly used for deciding when to formally undertake the risk process in a project. Each major activity within the project starts with a review, when the overall scope of the major activity is defined. Figure 8 shows where risk assessment can be embedded in this model.

The use of review and risk assessment processes can then be used to ensure the development is focused and controlled such that there is continual progress being made towards the desired outcome.

The GEMINI model (used initially for development of knowledge based systems – typically combining high risk and complexity) shows how risk and project management can be seen as a spiral model (Figure 9).

Resources for carrying out the various parts of the risk process should be prioritised and scheduled, so that detailed risk analysis is carried out in areas of greatest need rather than on all areas to the same level.

Communication

If each project produces a Summary Risk Profile (SRP), these can be used to show which projects are exposed to more risk. It should also assist in identifying common risk and communicating across the organisation at this level. The example in Figure 10 shows eight

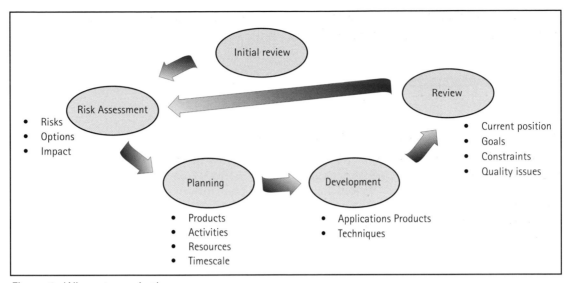

Figure 8: Where to apply the process

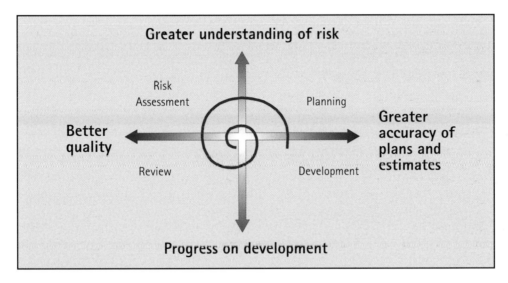

Figure 9: Spiral model

projects running in the organisation; some work together as part of programmes (the three groups); some communicate directly even though part of different programmes.

Within a programme there should be commonality across the projects in how they consider and report on risk. This will enable exchange of information between the individual projects in the way risk severity is defined and at the programme level.

SRPs can be difficult to interpret, as definitions of the severity of probability and impact may not be identical on different projects. The communication issues become more complex as you consider all levels of the organisation and how risk is evaluated at each.

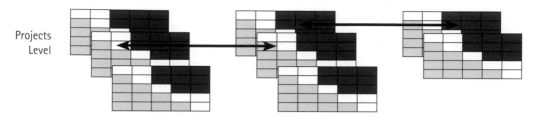

Projects
Level

Figure 10: Summary Risk Profiles at project level

The following example is intended to show some of the communication issues that arise when the risk process is implemented at each level of the organisation.

Example

Corporate strategy is to develop new business service based upon an e-commerce platform.

Risk framework is used to control the development and implementation of the new strategy and provide means of communicating information on risk.

Three key programmes have been established to implement strategy.

Projects are then established under major programmes, e.g.:

- applications development
- infrastructure
- architecture replacement
- security/business continuity management
- staff recruitment
- staff retraining
- office relocation
- customer relationship management.

The operational environment will change significantly, but has to maintain business as usual through the period of sustained change. Projects will be delivered at different times requiring a replacement or updating of existing technology, facilities and staff.

There is significant interdependency between the different programmes, and some high-level risks from certain projects have been escalated to the programme level.

The slippage of two key projects at the same time, combined with potential cost escalation, is escalated to the programme risk profiles and then to the strategic level as this threatens the benefits and delivery of the strategy.

Planned changes to the scope of the strategy are reported down to the programme and project levels.

The projects are creating risks to the operational environment, impacting on maintenance of legacy systems, changes to targets for new disaster recovery facilities and relocation of staff.

Further information about tools

For further information about selection of tools to support the management of risk process, see Annex K.

ANNEX A: EXAMPLES OF BENEFITS OF RISK MANAGEMENT

The following list of benefits should be applicable, at least in part, to any organisation and any situation.

A1   Strategic benefits

- Corporate decision making is improved through the high visibility of risk exposure, both for individual activities, and major projects, across the whole of the organisation.

- A progressive management style and a culture of continuous improvement are enhanced by the encouragement of openness in relation to risk.

- The organisation's image in the eyes of managers, major stakeholders, partners, suppliers and the public is enhanced through the visible and highly professional approach.

- Ensures that threats to cost, time and performance are managed with the clear aim of meeting the objectives of the organisation and its stakeholders.

- Creates an awareness of the risks in making business decisions at all levels in the organisation.

- Embedding the processes provides a clear message and directive in meeting the needs of corporate governance.

- Clear ownership and accountability for risk and its management.

- Enhances an awareness of the balance between costs and benefits which should lead to making appropriate business and operational decisions.

A2   Financial benefits

- Provides financial benefit to the organisation through improved 'value for money' potential.

- Improves management of project finance.

- Provides visibility and strict management of contingency plans.

A3   Programme benefits

- Management of project risk is carried out within the wider context of programmes, thus minimising the risk of individual project failure through the impact of other projects.

- Consistency of approach can be achieved throughout the programme by high-level monitoring and direction.

- Forward thinking is promoted throughout the programme, fostering greater confidence in project and programme success through commitment to risk management activities.

- A culture of openness and teamwork is generated through the collective participation in identification, management and reporting of risk activities.

- A wide range of data may be collected for detailed analysis, enhancing the ability to forecast outcomes and provide accurate estimates.

- Clarity of vision is engendered for uncertain or unknown work challenges, via the use of structured management of risk techniques.

- The organisation is prepared for most eventualities, and being assured of adequate contingency plans.

A4   Business process benefits

- Improves likelihood of supporting the agenda for the organisation as laid down by major stakeholders such as top management.

- Improves understanding of the project through the identification of risks and proper consideration of mitigation strategies.

- Creates an understanding of the relationship between risks, cost, programme timescale and price.

- Creates an environment for the conscious acceptance of business risks on an informed basis.

- Assists in the establishment of criteria for the inclusion of risk contingency.

- Reduces the need for costs to be hidden within individual elements of the cost estimate.

- Demonstrates clear corporate governance procedures.

A5   Overall management benefits

- Facilitates 'ownership' of both risks and their causes, so that they are effectively monitored, and proactively managed.

- Provides management with clear visibility of the risk and actions being taken to resolve them.

- Makes the relative importance of each risk immediately apparent.

- Improves contingency plans and the organisation's business continuity plans.

- Enables decision making to be more systematic and less subjective.

- Reduces the need for time or cost escalation.

- Reduces product performance shortfalls and maintenance expenditure.

- Brings realism into consideration of the trade-offs between performance, cost and time.

- Allows comparison of the robustness of projects to specific uncertainties.

- Assists in moving towards a 'no surprises' environment and so managing expectations.

- Facilitates selection of options alongside consideration of the fallback positions.

- Emphasises to project teams the importance of clear criteria for performance measurement.

- Provides a framework for encouraging lateral thinking in searching for better ways to mitigate risks.

- Creates an open and candid approach to risks that encourages the staff to assist in overcoming them.

- Encourages a considered and decisive style of management, resulting in proactive decisions and proper handling of the risks themselves, rather than later reactive decision making (management of crisis).

- Filters and prioritises risks so that management may have clear visibility of the important risks.

- Provides for acceptance and ownership of risks at the correct management level.

- Creates awareness in all personnel of the cost and benefit implications of their actions in managing risk.

ANNEX B: HEALTHCHECK: HOW WELL IS YOUR ORGANISATION MANAGING RISK?

NOTE: This checklist can be used from different perspectives such as:

- when preparing for, or carrying out internal and external risk audits

- when considering a new initiative, such as a major project, entering a new aquisition lifecycle

- when progress reporting to the management board or major stakeholders

- when preparing to raise commitment to improving the existing process

- before, or during Gateway Reviews.

B1   Key elements

Elements needed for an effective management of risk process and the indicators of a successful process include:

- policies for the management of risk and the benefits of effective risk management are clearly communicated to staff

- senior management support, promote, own and lead on risk management

- there is an organisational culture that supports well thought-through risk taking and innovation

- management of risk is fully embedded in the management process of the organisation, including the associated controls and distribution of management information

- the identification and assessment of risk is aimed at actively managing the key risks to the achievement of objectives

- the risks posed by working with other organisations are assessed.

B2   Review of overall effectiveness

- Is management of risk implemented across the organisation to all line management and business management, as well as project and programme management?

- Is there a formal documented policy for the management of risk? Does the policy address the following:

  - the corporate view of risk management?

  - processes and procedures?

  - the desired benefits to be achieved?

  - roles and responsibilities?

- facilities/tools required?
- documentation standards?

- Is the management of risk policy regularly reviewed?

- Are business continuity and contingency plans in place in the event that risks result in adverse consequences?

  - Are these plans tested (regularly reviewed and retested)?
  - Are those responsible aware of their roles with regard to each plan?
  - Is there a clearly identified authority to make the decision to implement each of the plans?
  - Are copies of the plan held off-site? (and accessible in an emergency?)

- Is there increasing visibility of risk and appropriate communication to staff so they understand their responsibility for being alert to risks?

  - Are staff being trained or receiving guidance in risk management?
  - Are risks being raised to the appropriate level?
  - Are major risks assigned owners?
  - Are you applying existing approaches/practices to address risk problems?
  - Are you following the standard processes and procedure for addressing problems in managing risk?

- Is there clear identification of types/categories of risk?

- Are risk evaluation criteria clearly identified and articulated?

  - Are risk responsibilities assigned for reporting and managing identified risks?
  - Is the effectiveness of risk treatments monitored and reviewed?
  - Is there appropriate communication and consultation with others within your organisation and with stakeholders?

- Is the risk documentation appropriate?

  - Is the documentation consistent throughout?

- Where appropriate, are you following the risk profile model in accordance with Cabinet Office guidelines?

- Is risk management ongoing and integrated with other procedures?

B3   Checklist: risk ownership

- Have owners been allocated for all the various parts of the complete management of risk process?
- Are the various roles and responsibilities associated with ownership well defined?
- Do the individuals who have been allocated ownership actually have the authority and capability to fulfil their responsibilities? For example, suppliers may be tasked with risk ownership.
- Have the various roles and responsibilities been communicated and understood?
- Are the nominated owners appropriate and aware of their nomination?

- Is ownership reassessed on a periodic basis, or in the event of a change in the situation; and if necessary, can it be quickly and effectively reallocated?

- Do all risks, and where appropriate their mitigation actions, have clearly identified owners? Are these owners appropriate?

B4   Checklist on risk identification

- Has a clear policy on the application of a risk-oriented management process and the scope of risks to be addressed been set at the appropriate level?

- Has the scope for management of risk been directly linked to the context and objectives of the situation?

- Has this been agreed and clearly communicated from the outset?

- Is the risk policy reviewed regularly to ensure it is still appropriate – that is, are strategic objectives linked to those of the programmes, projects and operations?

- Have changes to the objectives of the situation been fed back into the risk process and linked back to the entries in the risk register?

- Does the management of risk process cater for all different types of risk?

- Has a full, comprehensive set of threats been identified? Can you demonstrate this?

- Has a range of appropriate identification approaches been adopted?

- Has an appropriate set of tools and techniques been identified and adopted for managing risk?

B5   Checklist: risk evaluation and assessment of the organisation's willingness to take on risk

- Has the level of analysis that is required to support the decision process been agreed from the outset, such as start of the project, acquisition lifecycle, etc?

- Is there a demonstrable correlation between the amount of time, effort and cost expended in risk analysis to the difficulty in obtaining decisions, resources and funding for risk management, etc?

- Is the level of analysis, where possible, commensurate with the level of risk? For example, are detailed assessments of probabilities being carried out on threats that are known to have little, or no, impact?

- Is a consistent approach being taken to assessing potential impact, probability and possible action?

- Is there a good understanding of the relationship between the potential impact and the probability of the risk occurring?

- Is the risk information required communicated effectively to support the necessary decision making process, in a timely, clear and cost effective manner?

- Is there a clear understanding of the difference between a problem/issue management process and the risk process, and is there a suitable means of transferring from one to the other?

- Is there an understanding and commitment as to what level of risk is acceptable for a project, and the ability to communicate this? Does this reflect the potential for accruing benefits?

- Are the appropriate skills required to carry out the analysis available?

- Are risks being understated or overstated when assessed or evaluated, whether for commercial, political or individual reasons?

- Is there adequate commitment at all levels to the process of analysing and evaluating the threats? How was this established and are mechanisms in place to maintain commitment?

- Is the process of analysing and evaluating the threats sufficiently flexible to be able to respond to rapid change? For example, e-commerce developments increasingly require IT developers or other parts of the business, such as business relationship management, human resources, facilities etc., to gear up to deliver a solution to the 'market' within abnormally tight timescales.

- Is there a demonstrable correlation between the planned risk management activities (including assessment) and the risk to the level of exposure that it could engender?

- Is a consistent approach being taken regarding the identification and prioritisation of the risks in the risk management process and in any associated issue management process?

B6   Checklist: risk response

- Have the treatment measures recommended been assessed in terms of:
  - costs compared with the anticipated benefits of treating the risk?
  - the range of responses available?
  - the effectiveness in containing the risk or enhancing the opportunity?

- Do the risks have an adequate description that can be fully understood?

- Have the risks been assessed and prioritised to see which needs tackling first?

- Has the subsequent required treatment been set and agreed?

- Has there been a clear allocation of responsibilities and ownership for actions, decisions etc. and the required timescales for completion and review?

- Has the information required for communicating been identified, i.e., to whom, where, when and how?

- Is there a mechanism in place for monitoring and reporting on the effectiveness of the actions being undertaken?

- Has adequate contingency been planned to maintain the risk exposure within the designated risk tolerance level?

B7 Checklist: monitoring and control mechanisms

- Has appropriate ownership of the status reporting mechanism been achieved (that is, how it will be used, when and by whom as the owners and expeditors of that process)?

- Has the organisation put in place mechanisms to monitor the adequacy of processes required to ensure that cultural, political and personal pressures do not hinder truthful representation of status of high-profile risks?

- Is there confidence in the accuracy of reporting?

- Is the level of commitment to the reporting process adequate or is there a lack of commitment?

- When assessing and reporting effectiveness are the statements made factual rather than speculative?

ANNEX C: CATEGORISING RISK

C1   Threats and impacts

To analyse impact and probability you need to consider both the threats (sources) and effects of risk. One threat may give rise to several effects and there may be several threats which result in any particular effect. In addition, a 'domino effect' is highly probable; this is when the impact of one risk becomes the threat of further risk(s). Each of these subsequent threats needs to be analysed and appropriate responses considered.

When identifying risk you should think in terms of the following, or similar, phrase to express the risk in terms of threat and impact (or cause and effect)

'There is a risk of/that .... which may result in ....'

or

'There is a threat of .... which may result in ....'

Most risk will have the potential to lead to a detrimental effect on costs, timescales or the quality of the outcome (here operational concerns should be considered and addressed by the project if appropriate). By concentrating on the threats you are more likely to be able to take action that would reduce the impact.

There are a wide number of available promptlists to help you to categorise risk. These should be adapted to individual circumstances. This annex gives examples of promptlists that can be used to help an organisation consider the areas of most concern.

C2   Strategic risk – major threats

Sources of threat that may give rise to significant strategic risks include:

- budgeting (relates to availability or allocation of resources)
- fraud or theft
- unethical dealings
- product and/or service failure (resulting in lack of support to business processes; see example in Section 2.4)
- public perception and reputation
- lack of business focus
- exploitation of workers and/or suppliers (availability and retention of suitable staff)
- environmental (mis)management (issues relating to fuel consumption, pollution, etc.)
- occupational health and safety mismanagement and/or liability

- failure to comply with legal and regulatory obligations; and/or contractual aspect (can you sue or be sued?)

- civil action

- failure of the infrastructure (including utility supply systems, computer networks etc.)

- failure to address economic factors (such as interest rates, inflation, exchange rates)

- political and market factors (e.g. for management of risk, security, etc.)

- operational procedures – adequate and appropriate

- information/communication – adequate and appropriate

- capability to innovate (to exploit opportunities)

- failure to control intellectual property (e.g. as a result of abuse or industrial espionage)

- failure to take account of widespread disease or illness among the workforce

- failure to complete to published deadlines or timescales

- failure to take on new technology where appropriate to achieve objectives

- failure to invest appropriately

- failure to control IT effectively

- failure to establish a positive culture following business change

- vulnerability of resources (material and people)

- failure to establish effective contingency arrangements in the event of a product and/or service failure

- failure to establish effective continuity arrangements in the event of a disaster

- inadequate insurance/contingency provision

- disasters such as fire, flood, building subsidence, bomb incident.

C3 Threats to projects or programmes

The categories below can be used as a starting point for identifying your organisation's main areas of risk in relation to projects or programmes.

Corporate/commercial risks

- Under-performance to specification

- Management's underperformance against expectations

- Contractors go out of business

- Insolvency of financiers

- Failure of suppliers to meet contractual requirements; this could be in terms of quality, quantity, timescales or their own exposure to risk

- Insufficient capital revenues

- Market fluctuations
- Fraud/theft
- Partnerships failing to deliver the desired outcome
- The situation being non-insurable (or cost of insurance outweighs the benefit)
- Lack of availability of capital investment.

Economic/financial/market risks

- Exchange rate fluctuation
- Interest rate instability
- Inflation
- Shortage of working capital
- Failure to meet projected revenue targets
- Market developments will adversely affect plans.

Legal and regulatory risks

- New, or changed, legislation may invalidate assumptions upon which the activity is based
- Failure to obtain appropriate approval such as planning consent
- Unforeseen inclusion of contingent liabilities
- Loss of intellectual property rights
- Failure to achieve satisfactory contractual arrangements (further discussion in Annex E)
- Unexpected regulatory controls or licensing requirements
- Changes in tax or tariff structure
- Infringement of personal data protection criteria.

Organisational management/human factors

- Management incompetence
- Inadequate corporate policies
- Inadequate adoption of management practices
- Poor leadership
- Key personnel who have inadequate authority to fulfil their roles
- Poor staff selection procedures
- Lack of clarity over roles and responsibilities
- Vested interests creating conflict and compromising the overall aims
- Individual or group interests will be given unwarranted priority
- Personality clashes

- Indecision or inappropriate decision making

- Inadequate management of expectations

- Lack of operational support

- Inadequate or inaccurate information

- Health and safety compromised – for example:

  - working environment presents physical dangers

  - staff under stress for significant, sustained periods.

Political/societal factors

- Change of government policy (national or international)

- Change of government

- War and disorder

- Adverse public opinion/media intervention.

Environmental factors/Acts of God (force majeure)

- Natural disasters

- Storms, floods, etc.

- Pollution incidents

- Transport problems, including aircraft/vehicle collisions.

Technical/operational/infrastructure risks

- Inadequate design

- Professional negligence

- Human error/incompetence

- Infrastructure failure

- Operational lifetime shorter than expected

- Residual value of assets lower than expected

- Increased dismantling/decommissioning costs

- Safety being compromised

- Performance failure (people or equipment)

- Residual maintenance problems

- Scope creep

- Unclear expectations/objectives

- Breaches in physical security/information security

- Lack or inadequacy of business continuity and contingency measures with regard to this activity

- Unforeseen barriers or constraints due to infrastructure.

C4 Operational risks

Aspects to consider here include:

- lack of clarity of service requirements

- inadequate infrastructure to provide required operational services

- inadequate or inappropriate people available to support the required service provision

- inappropriate contract in place and/or inadequate contract management to support required level of service provision

- changing requirements, enabled in an uncontrolled way

- products passed to operational teams without due consideration to implementation, handover and subsequent maintenance, decommissioning

- unexpected or inappropriate expectations of service users

- inadequate incident handling

- lack or inadequacy of business continuity or contingency measures with regard to maintaining (critical) business services

- lack of investment in infrastructure to support future needs/opportunities

- failing to meet legal or contractual obligations.

ANNEX D: SETTING A STANDARD FOR EVALUATION OF RISK

This annex describes some ways of looking at risk so that its severity can be evaluated; it includes use of the Summary Risk Profile (described in Chapter 8), and additional criteria to consider in relation to the Summary Risk Profile.

The validity of the estimate of the severity of a risk is directly related to several factors, including:

- the accuracy of historical information
- experience (skill and competency) of personnel and any personal bias
- any ambiguity over the terms of reference for the analysis.

D1   Using the Summary Risk Profile

Within this guide, the Summary Risk Profile uses five levels for the probability (or likelihood) of a risk occurring, and impact of a risk. The five levels are:

- very low
- low
- medium
- high
- very high.

Another approach would be to use a numeric scale, e.g. 1 to 10.

The definitions below are intended to provide a common understanding of what is meant by these terms for different aspects of the risk (probability and impact). The scales shown are to illustrate how the scales might be set. These scales will need to be adjusted to suit the needs of individual activities. Another aspect of risk is the 'proximity'. This relates to when the impact might occur, as the severity of the impact will usually change over time.

D2   Looking at probability

Probability of occurrence can be difficult for 'risk-takers' to understand, particularly when trying to assess the significance of the probability. Trying to put numbers to five categories (such as low) helps to give people a common understanding of risk exposure.

It should be recognised that a threat which has little impact is unlikely to be directly assessed, no matter how likely it is to occur. This will be a significant aspect of the analysis. A threat with a zero probability will never happen and therefore presents no threat. A threat that is 100% certain to happen is not a risk but an issue (or problem) that you have to address. So, in terms of risk management, you are looking for threats whose probability lies within these extremes.

The chance of a threat having an impact is illustrated with the situation of starting new business ventures. For example, there could be a 90% probability of new businesses failing at start-up; if there are ten attempts at starting up a business, only one of them is likely to succeed. If there is a 50% probability of failure, the ten attempts would result in five successful new business start-ups.

The types of value shown in Tables 12, 13 and 14 below could be stated for probability:

Table 12

Very low	0 to 0.1
Low	0.1 to 0.2
Medium	0.2 to 0.5
High	0.5 to 0.8
Very high	0.8 to 1

Table 13

Very low	Virtually impossible: 0 to 5%
Low	Low but not impossible: 6 to 20%
Medium	Fairly likely to occur: 21 to 50%
High	More likely to occur than not: 51% to 80%
Very high	> 81%

Table 14

Very low	less than 10 out of 100
Low	from 10 to 19 out of 100
Medium	from 20 to 49 out of 100
High	from 50 to 79 out of 100
Very high	80 or more out of 100

D3   Looking at impact

Impacts on an activity are usually considered in terms of effect on costs, scheduling (timing and resourcing) and quality (ability to meet objectives or support critical success factors). Each of these will need to be defined in terms of appropriateness to the activity. Some will have current limits that are quite low, but there will always be an initial plan and business case, and the impacts are measured against the information set out in those documents.

The ranges should be selected to suit the project, organisation or situation, and also take into consideration the business sensitivity in terms of successful outcome. The cost example in Table 15 is more likely to apply to larger organisations. Small organisations with less funding will need to consider their own levels for this type of impact.

Table 15: Cost impact

Very low	£0 to £25,000
Low	£25,000 to £100,000
Medium	£100,000 to £400,000
High	£400,000 to £800,000
Very high	£800,000 to £1,000,000

Given an overall acceptable budget it may be appropriate to calculate risk factors using that budget as a basis to work from. Table 16 provides an example:

Table 16: Budgetary impact

Very low	Negligible effect on projected cost: cost 0 to 3%
Low	Small increase: 3 to 10%
Medium	Significant increase: 10 to 30%
High	Large increase: 30 to 75%
Very high	Major increase: > 75%

Table 17 looks at impact on project schedule:

Table 17: Schedule impact

Very low	No effect on projected schedule: < 3%
Low	Small schedule slip: 3 to 10%
Medium	Significant slip: 10 to 30%
High	Large delay: 30 to 50%
Very high	Major delay: > 50%

Table 18 shows an example of a project whose development activity is estimated at six months, but whose end date is not a critical part of the requirement:

Table 18: Schedule impact where time is not critical

Very low	Less than two days' delay
Low	Small schedule slip: less than two weeks
Medium	Significant slip: between two weeks and two months
High	Large delay: between two and three months
Very high	Major delay: three months or more

Table 19 is a further example of a project whose end date is a critical part of the requirement (i.e. delay in delivery is not acceptable). Here any delay may be considered to be very high risk or the following categorisation may be used to help identify potential responses against this impact of the risk.

Table 19: Schedule impact where time is a critical factor

Very low	N/A
Low	N/A
Medium	Significant slip: up to one day
High	Large delay: between two and five days
Very high	Major delay: one week or more

It may also be considered a risk if the project finishes too early as this may compromise the quality of the end product. Thus it may be appropriate to look at early delivery in these terms as well as delay (as shown above).

Finally, Table 20 investigates technical performance in relation to requirement:

Table 20: Impact on requirements

Very low	System will fully meet mandatory requirements
Low	A few shortfalls in desirable functionality
Medium	Minor shortfalls in one or more key requirements
High	Major shortfalls in one or more key parameters
Very high	Major shortfall in any of the critical requirements

No quantitative equivalents are shown for these performance measures as they will depend on the application and development strategy. Appropriate values may be defined on the basis of a project's particular requirements.

Warning

Using a three-point scale can be dangerous as it may be difficult to decide which risks are significant and warrant attention. The Summary Risk Profile as proposed uses a five-point scale but use of a 10 point scale may be beneficial. Within some organisations it may be decided to use a four-point scale such as *low, moderate, significant* and *catastrophic*. In this example, risks that are significant or catastrophic must be addressed; low or moderate risks must be monitored but do not have to be subjected to reduction action.

Impact categories in particular will vary in effect across the organisation. Typically a small impact to a project will be negligible to the organisation as a whole (unless it is part of a business critical project). Board considerations will be focused on profitability, ongoing viability, reputation, competitiveness, regulatory compliance and stakeholder perceptions (values) rather than cost, time, quality.

ANNEX E: PROCUREMENT, CONTRACTUAL AND LEGAL CONSIDERATIONS

Any major undertaking for an organisation will require resources: skilled people, and equipment. Frequently these resources will not be available from within the organisation and require a procurement exercise to obtain them externally.

Figure 2 in Chapter 2 shows the acquisition lifecycle, which includes procurement and the subsequent setting up and maintenance of contracts. EC legislation covers these activities to ensure that procurements are conducted in a fair and reasonable manner and that supporting contracts are appropriate.

You should use specialists to advise on the legal issues concerning procurement and contracts; this Annex sets out the general principles.

E1   Modular and incremental approaches

Key areas of threats to be considered during procurements include:

- commercial viability of the relationship. Fixed price contracts, in theory, transfer risk to the provider as they estimate the severity of the threat posed. But a provider who underbids may underperform (or in extreme cases abandon the contract) and have little incentive to improve its performance if it sees no way of making a profit. Procurement teams must therefore ensure that proposed deals are viable for the provider.

- failure to allocate responsibility for the different aspects of business change. By default such responsibility will remain with the customer organisation and any failures to manage necessary business change (whether the requirements for it are referred to explicitly in the contract or not) will usually amount to a breach of contract by the customer organisation entitling the provider to extensions of time and/or damages for its additional delay costs.

- adequacy of drafting requirements (e.g. systems specifications or service level agreements). These document the current requirement, but are rarely drafted with the necessary rigour to enable them to form a sound baseline for change control. Frequently these receive very little legal/commercial scrutiny. Without a clear requirement there is likely to be 'scope creep' which often results in time and cost overruns.

- clarifying the commercial relationship as part of contractual documentation. This area of the contract should make it clear which roles and responsibilities relate to the customer and the provider so that these can then be appropriately undertaken. Each party should be aware of their commitments and understand their liabilities so they are in a position to accept and manage these.

PFI contracts can be used to procure modular and incremental work. This can be done by using a single provider and contracting to that one provider for specific modules and increments. In certain circumstances it will be possible to open certain modules to competition and introduce an additional provider.

The Treasury Task Force has found that 'pay as you go' contracts for major software development had more success in terms of being completed to time and budget. In recognition of this finding, PFI contracts for incremental and modular work should provide for the contractor to receive some revenue earlier than the date planned for full implementation. Milestone payments, linked to delivery of increments, can provide such revenue for the contractor, and give them incentives to manage delivery to target.

When evaluating provider proposals, it is important to consider the effects of the size and nature of business that they are being asked to support. Adopting an incremental or modular approach should make it easier for you to deploy specialist providers on specific aspects of the acquisition, but you will need to address the practicalities of integrating the deliverables as a coherent whole – perhaps by appointing a lead provider.

Which risks are transferable?

A major tenet of the government's Private Finance Initiative (PFI) is to allocate service and project risks (delivery to budget, to time and to quality) to the party best placed to manage them. It is important to recognise which risks cannot be transferred to the private sector.

There are some mechanisms which can be adopted to assist with transferral of risk including joint ventures (with shared responsibility for risk) and taking out insurance cover. Note that you cannot transfer business risk.

Purchase of preparatory work

During the pre-contract phase, one mechanism that can help to firm up requirements is the use of prototypes. It is important to clarify the purpose of a prototype before adopting such an approach.

Most prototypes are throwaway systems that are built as cheaply as possible to help clarify requirements, or to prove a concept.

Prototyping is defined as the development of a preliminary version of part, or all, of a design concept to allow various aspects of that design to be investigated (which could be for a product, a service, a building and so on). A prototype is used to firm up requirements or when requirements are clear and to obtain feedback from the intended users. Prototyping forms the basis of the end result. User feedback is reflected in the analysis and design, increasing user confidence in the final system. A prototype can be used to investigate problem areas of the implications of other options.

The benefits of prototyping include:

- clarification of requirements
- gaining user commitment
- improving developer understanding
- speeding up the development process

- verification of designs
- automation of specifications
- checking feasibility
- elicitation of requirements.

By purchasing preparatory work, an organisation can reduce its risks, and better inform itself and its providers of the requirements.

Areas to study/prototype

- Business process design; implementation plan; service description; technical interface design with other linked developments
- Reports used to confirm understanding of the requirements and allow the organisation to assess the viability of the provider's proposals.

E2   Contract risk management

This area of an acquisition is likely to prove critical to the success of the undertaking because:

- the contractual relationship with a key provider may be the primary means of implementing strategy and achieving specific objectives (programme, project or operational)
- the contract is a means of allocating and managing most, if not all, operational risks associated with the desired outcome (delivery of a particular service or successful outcome for the project).

Poor specifications are the most frequent single, immediate cause of contractual disputes. OGC provides guidance on procurement and contractual matters – see 'Further information' for more details.

If a contract covers work to be delivered incrementally, it must allow the purchaser to stop development, or change direction, in a controlled way which is understood by the provider.

The requirements for a module/increment must be capable of being expressed clearly and unambiguously. No element of the existing requirement should be defined post-contract. Changes in requirements should only be dealt with through a clearly identified, robust change mechanism.

Modular and incremental contracts can allow contractors to receive some revenue earlier than would be the case if the implementation were to be carried out all at once, for example, through making milestone payments which are linked to delivery of increments. To achieve this, the recommended approach is for there to be a pre-procurement phase, during which the organisation spends time considering the exact nature of the project, and how its implementation will help them to meet their business objectives.

During the contract documentation phase, the requirements should be specified in terms that are full, clear and unambiguous, and capable of measurement (to facilitate performance monitoring). In addition, both these requirements and the contractor's technical solution should be set out in the contract itself.

E3　Outsourcing to support business needs

When an activity is wholly or partially outsourced there are implications for the management of risk for both the owner organisation and the service provider. When considering outsourcing both organisations need to reflect on the following questions:

- What risks exist? (that is, what can stop you achieving your objectives?)
- Are individual risks increased, decreased or just different as a result of outsourcing?
- Who, or what, is threatened by a risk and who can take action to ameliorate that risk?
- Who is, or should be, responsible for managing the risk?

Table 21 shows the major issues that the owner (customer) needs to consider in an outsourcing situation.

Who resolves the issues?

The customer organisation is responsible for ensuring that the right level of information is collected from all parties to enable a true assessment of risk to be made. To enable risk exposure to the outsourcing to be reduced the parties need to agree who is responsible for managing particular risks and accept that responsibility. Arrangements for managing risk must be documented in the contract.

E4　Legal aspects of procurement

This is a highly specialised area of law and most organisations have legal advisers who can assist in ensuring these areas are adequately covered. This section looks briefly at some of the major legal issues of procurement but is not intended to be a substitute for more specialist support.

Breach of contract

By late provisions of information or other failures to co-operate with the provider, the customer organisation may expose itself to risks that:

- the contractor is entitled to an extension of time for completion
- any entitlement to liquidated damages is lost
- the contractor is entitled to claim damages from the customer for its own delay costs.

Table 21: Risk issues to consider, from the customer perspective, when outsourcing

Focus	Considerations (is there a risk that...)
Business needs	<ul><li>you do not have a clear view of your future business needs or will lose control of the strategic direction of the outsourcing?</li><li>the original business objectives will stop being the focus for the service provision?</li><li>you will lose control of your information?</li><li>trends in the business environment will not be adequately monitored and reacted to?</li></ul>
Management and control	<ul><li>the requirements are poorly defined, incomplete or inconsistent, or prescribe how the requirements must be met?</li><li>use of innovative ideas will be inhibited?</li><li>no thought will be given to procedures which need to be operable at the end of the contractual period?</li></ul>
Procurement, relationship management	<ul><li>the procurement procedures are too restrictive?</li><li>the contract will be inflexible, too restricted?</li><li>the provider's performance will be difficult to monitor and accurately measure?</li><li>responsibilities and roles will not be clearly defined?</li><li>provider lock-in can occur?</li></ul>
Other, e.g. human resource	<ul><li>there will be deficiencies in culture/customer relations?</li><li>there will be a loss of in-house expertise (leading to inability to manage the contract effectively)?</li></ul>

Privacy law

Disclosure of personal confidential information, not just commercial confidential information, can expose the organisation to the risk of legal action for infringement of the common law of confidence. This applies in addition to data protection legislation. This area also needs to consider the areas of damage to reputation and defamation, against individuals as well as business interests.

Public procurement rules

There are general rules of procurement, but the public sector has to be able to prove it makes appropriate use of public funds. To support this there are various sets of public procurement legislation. Breach of these regulations exposes the organisation to the risks of:

- injunction
- court action for damages
- setting aside of contracts
- the aborting of a procurement process and the obligation to restart the entire process form scratch or else abandon the procurement.

The severity of the risk of a particular infringement will depend on the degree of the infringement and the loss suffered by the aggrieved provider and can only be accurately assessed by a specialist legal adviser.

Other legal/regulatory areas

Additional areas to consider as a minimum include:

- Treaty of Rome
- a buying consortium or electronic marketplace system may infringe competition rules in contravention of the Competition Act 1998 or Articles 81 and 82 of the Treaty of Rome
- TUPE, pensions or transfer of staff
- occupier's liability, health and safety for use of premises
- product liability, tort (negligence) for causing death or personal injury
- infringement of intellectual property rights (IPR), including copyright and trademarks/passing off – this may be dealt with within the contractual terms and conditions
- commercial ventures or financial arrangements may be *ultra vires*.

ANNEX F: BUSINESS CONTINUITY MANAGEMENT

F1   Why is business continuity management important?

You must have plans in place to cope with disasters such as terrorist attack and fire damage or failure to implement business change as planned. Having a business continuity plan is good management practice and supports the aims and needs of good corporate governance. Business continuity planning can help to identify the critical areas which need to be preserved and so increase the chances of surviving for the future. As part of that good practice these plans should be developed, maintained, regularly 'practised' and reviewed for effectiveness.

The existence of business continuity plans should be covered within the 'risk management framework' for the organisation. If these plans are generated in isolation from that document there will be inconsistencies that may cause significant problems at an operational level should a business continuity plan be invoked.

This annex outlines good practice in relation to business continuity management. It highlights the need to revisit business continuity plans regularly, at least annually, if such plans are to have any ongoing value to the organisation.

F2   What is business continuity management?

Many of the terms associated with business continuity are used interchangeably. Key terms used in this guidance are:

Business continuity and business continuity management

> Looking at the totality of the organisation: what services and processes are vital to ensure the business can survive into the future? This includes derivation and integration of the planning cycle into business operations and the subsequent evaluation of any business continuity measures adopted.

Business continuity planning

> Looking at the totality of the organisation, identify what can go wrong with those elements that must function for the business to survive. This includes building a plan of action which is to be instigated as specific circumstances arise. It is also vital to maintain awareness of any changes in the business environment that require the plans to be updated so that they remain valid and applicable.

Contingency planning

> Concentrates on one particular element (e.g. a project, or a programme, or a contract, or provision of IT service) of the organisation. With that element in mind, define the appropriate protection measures to maintain that element within the

parameters set by management. So a business continuity plan is likely to be supported by several contingency plans.

Disaster recovery planning

A series of processes that focus upon recovery processes, principally in response to physical disasters. This forms part of business continuity planning, not the totality.

Other definitions to be aware of are those developed by the Home Office emergency planning division:

'Emergency planning'

The work, normally led by emergency planners, in planning how to handle civil emergencies.

'Contingency planning'

The means by which organisations plan to handle incidents that might adversely affect the operation of their organisation.

'Business continuity planning'

The means by which organisations plan to maintain their business in the event of damage to critical elements of that business.

F3 How to implement business continuity management

There is a four-stage lifecycle for business continuity management, outlined below.

Stage 1: Initiation (a strategic-level activity)

- Sets the policy and scope for business continuity management
- Establishes the business continuity management initiative.

Stage 2: Requirements and strategy

- Assesses potential business impacts and risks
- Identifies and evaluates options
- Develops a cost effective strategy. This strategy must balance real business priorities against the risks of failing to provide functionality against costs of adopting particular business continuity options.

Stage 3: Implementation

- Establishes a programme for achieving business continuity
- Implements the business continuity management strategy
- Undertakes initial testing of the business continuity plan.

Stage 4: Operational management/recovery

- Maintains the strategy, plans and procedures

- During this stage you need to look at education and awareness, review of the plans and risks (with their associated reduction measures), testing of the plans, controlling changes to the strategy and the plans so these are maintained to be consistent with each other

- Training of people to produce the strategy and plans as well as to undertake the actions embodied within the plans

- There is an overall need to assure the quality and applicability of the plans. In this context 'quality' refers to adaptability, completeness, data quality, efficiency, friendliness/usability (very important as the plan will only be used in a time of chaos or disaster), maintainability, portability, reliability, resilience, security, testability and timeliness.

Recovery of normal operations needs to be the final – and planned for – objective of business continuity management.

F4   Structuring business continuity plans

Business continuity plans (BCPs) need to cover the whole organisation. To assist with usability it helps to structure the plans based on the types of threats (boundaries) the plan covers. The organisation needs to look in three main areas:

- supporting the business for itself (looking internally at the business processes and systems and externally at how these are supported by suppliers and customers)

- locally and nationally – what contribution do you make to the community, economy, essential services, etc?

- internationally – what support do you need to give, and receive, in this arena?

Each of these areas may be built up from specific plans that combine to address one particular area, but those needs will be specific to your organisation.

Business managers must decide what is critical, plan for how this can be supported and agree this with top management. 'Critical' in this context is based on assessing which business functions are required to ensure your organisation survives. Thus focusing on maintaining services to customers is usually the primary concern, at least in the short term. If a situation becomes protracted, ensuring maintenance of supplies to your organisation and concerns with cashflow will begin to dominate the BCP requirements. Your suppliers' role in these activities must also be considered and addressed as part of BCM. Decide on the primary role of the organisation and support that role.

Ensure that any assumptions made in planning are restated in the plans, as these will affect the decisions made and the applicability of the actions to be undertaken. In a time of crisis the documented plan may be the only information available to the people responding to the crisis – they need to understand the context of the plan.

F5   Business continuity supported by a risk management process

The business continuity process is essentially risk management applied to the whole organisation in a coherent, consistent manner. Throughout the business continuity lifecycle you need to ensure risk management is applied.

The basic risk management processes are used iteratively rather than a strict sequence. The risk management process is discussed in Chapter 3.

F6   Who to involve in business continuity management

Top management needs to endorse the BCPs for an organisation, as part of their responsibilities for corporate governance.

A nominated individual must have overall responsibility for the business continuity plan. As this is a plan relating to the survival of the whole organisation this needs to be a senior person who has sufficient authority to ensure things are done. While this person will 'own' the BCP, they may not be responsible for its production; they will require expert help.

Within individual plans there will be actions to counter specific risks. It is good practice to identify individuals to manage action against specific risks where instigation requires specific technical skills.

F7   Issues to consider in a BCP

By identifying the events that would trigger an action the timing of the contingency measures can be built in. This may also identify the latest acceptable dates for testing specific elements of plans. For example, if you are introducing a new service with IT support, your BCPs will need to be updated to reflect this change and become operational at the point the new service is implemented.

If, as part of your continuity measures, you decide to resort to a manual system in case of the IT support failing, consider the following:

● how long will it take to train the staff?

● what training will staff need over time if the BCP is not activated, so that they remain the required skills level?

● will paper forms need to be available, are these already printed and in store? How can they be produced or retrieved?

F8   Assuring your BCP is viable

Individual elements of each plan need to be tested (or practised or rehearsed). Final sign-off of a particular plan or element of a plan depends on when testing can be carried out. The level of testing and the degree to which this is a 'desk check' will depend on the nature of the problem being addressed and the level of detail included.

High level plans will not go to a level of detail where they identify individual actions and so will have to be 'desk checked' to ensure they are coherent, logical and practical. Individual detailed plans, to support the high-level ones, should be tested in a way that gives confidence that they will work in a crisis. In many cases a 'desk check' would not give the necessary degree of confidence. Another consideration here is the cost of undertaking these tests.

Tests are likely to disrupt the business in some form. When testing BCPs, issues to consider include:

- is it possible to time this testing to cause least disruption to your business functions or less upset to your customer?

- how much will the test cost? Is this appropriate for the additional confidence gained over other forms of testing, including a desk check?

- how can staff be trained to cope with the situation if they do not experience it in test-mode?

- once the BCP is in operation – how will you return to normal business operations? Are there specific issues here that warrant testing in their own right?

F9   Where to store BCPs

Business continuity plans should be accessible to the person who will use them. Back-up copies of all plans should be available in case the plan or the primary person is unavailable when the plan needs to be actioned. To be fully protected there should be a secondary contact for each plan that is to be actioned.

F10   Communications

Whenever there is a major disruption of services there is likely to be some media interest. The nature of your services is likely to dictate the degree of concern that is likely to arise amongst the customers of your services – this is of particular concern if your customers are 'the citizen'. It is important that all organisations, especially those in the public sector, do their best to allay concerns.

All organisations should therefore consider the needs of all stakeholders and actively explain their plans. This demonstrates that the risks to key services have been managed.

If disaster then strikes, your stakeholders will have some assurance that you have the capability to cope and so they are less likely to panic. If customers are very concerned they will try to contact the organisation. At a time of crisis this could use resources that the organisation may need to deploy on other activities to meet the needs of the crisis. Thus the more informed your stakeholders, the more control you have of your resources.

F11   BCM summary

The *key messages* to consider are:

- You must understand the primary business needs of your organisation (what services must you provide to survive?).

- Manage expectations of major stakeholders. These may be Board members, customers, the general public, or suppliers. Prepare them for what could happen and keep them informed. They need to know in advance the basis of your contingency plans and of particular concern will be communications over any 'period of crisis'.

- How prepared is your organisation? What can you NOT do?

- Business continuity planning comes from the high level and plans are refined with more detail as you get to the operational level.

- Identify key milestones that will trigger contingency actions and clearly define those actions.

- 'Business as usual' is not a likely option – but it can be aimed for with a structured path to show how you will 'resume normal operations' if things go wrong.

- Resources (time, skills, funds, and equipment) are limited. If things go wrong how will you make best use of available resources to maintain your primary business services?

- A major area of vulnerability is your dependence on others. It is essential to talk to suppliers, partners and customers to clarify these inter-dependencies.

- A business continuity plan is used in times of trouble – keep it simple and ensure it is available to the right people at the right time and that they know how to implement it.

ANNEX G: MANAGING ORGANISATIONAL SAFETY AND SECURITY

G1   How are safety and security related?

Safety and security are defined as follows:

- safety: the condition of being safe from harm

- security: the state of being secure (certain to remain safe). This can be interpreted as an adequate level of safety of the organisation against espionage, theft or other danger.

The same overall process for managing risk, as described in Chapter 3, can be applied to the management of safety and security. The main differences come from the frequency of:

- change of the various related issues

- review of the measures to address them.

The threats to safety and security tend to be fairly static in that they will apply over a long period of time. Measures to address them can be put in place and usually will be effective for a significant period of time. Safety issues are covered by legislation and so the need to comply is laid down externally. Some security measures address a specific technical issue and so when the technology is changed the applicability of the measures to protect them needs to be reviewed. An example might be access to buildings – unless you relocate or change any of the main systems controlling access then the security measures are likely to remain; the main issue here is to ensure that existing measures support the organisation in an appropriate way.

Maintenance of appropriate levels of safety and security should be documented such that staff understand such requirements and their responsibility for ensuring they are enforced. Indeed security management frequently covers some aspects relating to health and safety. The management of these aspects is closely related.

G2   Mandate for ensuring safety and security

It is good management practice to protect your investment from others. The most important asset of an organisation is the people, and so ensuring their safety is a major responsibility. Information is another major business asset and it needs to be suitably protected to ensure business continuity, minimise business damage and maximise Return on Investment and business opportunities. Today everyone is more dependent on technology in the management of their information and so the range of security issues that need to be considered is broadened.

Apart from the commercial reasons for protecting information, businesses have legal obligations to take care of personal information entrusted to them.

There is an increasing amount of legislation which is relevant to security, including:

- Data Protection Act (DPA) 1984 and 1998

- the Copyrights, Designs and Patents act 1988 (amended by DPA)

- Computer Misuse Act 1990

- Public Records Act 1958 and 1967

- Human Rights Act

- Electronic Communications Act

- Freedom of Information Act.

Health and safety legislation relates to all aspects of people within a working environment. This is a specialist area and requires adequate training as well as fully assigned responsibility for ensuring adequate controls are in place.

In the area of health, safety and welfare there are various regulations and sets of legislation. These include:

- Workplace (Health and Safety and Welfare) Regulations 1992

- buildings related regulations (for example, Electricity at work Regulations (1989) covering, among other things, ergonomics, lighting, noise levels and air quality)

- Fire Precautions (1997)

- Control of Hazardous Substances (1998)

- Working Time Regulations (1998 based on EU Working Time Directive)

- EU Part-time working Directive (2000).

- The Health and Safety Executive produce much guidance in this area including specific guidance on the prevention of work related illness. For further information consult their website at http://www.hse.gov.uk/

G3   Securing assets

Everyone within an organisation has a responsibility for security in some form. People need to understand that responsibility, level of accountability and the procedures that apply to them. The main areas that need to be considered for security purposes are:

- personnel

- physical

- document

- IT

- information.

There are overlaps between some of these categories – in particular, technical and document security. These overlaps may sometimes be difficult to clarify. BS7799 (ISO 17799) applies to the area of information security management. Key areas to consider are outlined below.

Personnel security

Organisations will wish to make arrangements to check staff and consultants that are to work for them. There may be different levels of clearance required for security purposes. The levels and circumstances to which they apply should be clearly documented. The required security check should be undertaken as part of the recruitment process. In many cases this will simply involve taking up a number of references. These references may relate to personal or business associations. Additionally, when a persons role within the organisation changes this may also require a change of clearance level.

Physical security

- *Access to buildings*: this should cover ensuring access at a business location; it should take account of the impact of fire, flood, terrorism, risks to transport infrastructure. It should also ensure that only authorised people gain access to the building or parts of the building. Arrangements should cover staff, consultants or other visitors.

- *Access to information*: only those people with appropriate authority are allowed access to the organisation's information. An important consideration is the Data Protection Act, which requires suitable controls for the handling of personal information.

- *Availability of resources*: people or equipment must be available at the right time and place to fulfil the business requirement. It should take account of the facilities people need and whether the building is adequately heated, supplied with water, sewerage systems and so on.

Document security

The Data Protection Act requires that:

'Appropriate security measures shall be taken against unauthorised access to, or alteration, disclosure or destruction of, personal data and against accidental loss or destruction of personal data.'

Documentation needs to be maintained to ensure confidentiality, availability and integrity.

Technical security

This aspect needs to consider the security requirements of technology related assets, in particular IT networks, systems and equipment. This has to be balanced with enabling staff to make appropriate use of equipment so they can perform their designated business function. Topics that require specific consideration for IT equipment include:

- use of internal networks
- Internet access
- e-mail
- viruses
- hacking
- remote working
- backing up information (particularly from laptops).

G4   Security incidents

A security incident is any deliberate or accidental event which leads to an actual or possible:

- breach of confidentiality – when information is disclosed to people who have no permission to have it

- breach of integrity – when access to information is changed without permission

- breach of availability – anything which restricts or hinders the ongoing business functionality.

There must be policies and proven procedures in place to deal with security incidents as they arise.

G5   Adopting good practice in information security management

Critical success factors for adopting information security management include:

- establishing a clear security policy, objectives and activities that reflect business objectives

- ensuring the policy is owned and supported by senior management

- building a good understanding of security risks (the threats, probability and impacts), ensuring this is based on the value and importance of the assets

- effective marketing of the security policy and associated issues to all managers and employees

- distribution of comprehensive guidance on the security policy and standards to all employees and contractors. Supported by appropriate training, this should ensure everyone understands their responsibilities and actively follows the guidance.

The British Standard, BS 7799, has been widely adopted as a business-led approach to best practice on information security management.

ANNEX H: INFORMATION ON FURTHER TECHNIQUES TO SUPPORT MANAGEMENT OF RISK

Table 22 shows a range of typical techniques and the risk activity for which they are best suited.

Table 22: Cross reference of techniques to the management of risk activities

Technique	Identification	Evaluation	Planning	Controlling	Monitoring
Cause-and-effect diagrams	✔	✔			
Cost/benefit analysis		✔	✔	✔	✔
Critical success factors and key focus areas	✔	✔	✔		
Decision trees	✔	✔	✔		
Insurance premium approach		✔	✔		
Library of previous experience	✔	✔			
Monte Carlo simulation		✔	✔	✔	
Probability/impact grids		✔		✔	
Radar charts				✔	✔
Risk checklists	✔				
Risk identification workshop	✔				
Risk management plan	✔	✔	✔	✔	✔
Risk management workshop		✔	✔		
Risk register	✔	✔	✔	✔	✔

It is frequently useful to be able to present the results of risk analysis in a simple way. *Probability and impact grids*, *scatter diagrams* and *radar charts* are typical examples. The choice of presentation may be made to suit the reporting requirements of the programme.

H1   Risk identification workshops

A risk identification workshop is a group session which is designed to focus on a particular aspect of an activity for the identification of risks. The aspect may be a particular phase of a programme or the possible effects of a particular cause of risk. Participants should reflect the views of all stakeholders in the activity.

For maximum benefit, potential attendees should be asked for some basic information as input to the workshop; the workshop should be facilitated by an experienced risk practitioner, who would employ particular identification techniques and share the benefit of in-depth programme and project experience. This would lead to a broad range of risks being identified with some view of possible risk owners.

The benefit of a group session is to:

- gather the necessary fields of expertise together

- speed the process of risk identification

- reach agreement by consensus.

Risk identification workshops are most effective as half-day sessions during which, if time allows, identified risks may also be estimated and evaluated.

H2   Risk management workshops

These workshops are similar to risk identification workshops but start with a clear view of threats which will then be considered in terms of how they can be addressed as well as agreeing the assessment of severity of the risk. Participants should also look for any secondary risks that may be raised.

Participants should include people who may be responsible for responding to risks and/or owning them.

H3   Cause-and-effect diagrams

Cause-and-effect diagrams, also known as fish-bone diagrams, are graphical representations of the causes of various events which lead to one or more impacts.

Each diagram may possess several start-points (A-points) and one or more end-points (B-points). Construction of the diagram may begin from an A-point and work towards a B-point or extrapolate backwards from a B-point. This is largely a matter of preference. Some people prefer to start with an impact (B-point) and work backwards to its cause. Others prefer to start with an event (A-point) and work towards an impact.

Figure 11 shows an example of a cause-and-effect diagram, which works back from a B-point to multiple A-points.

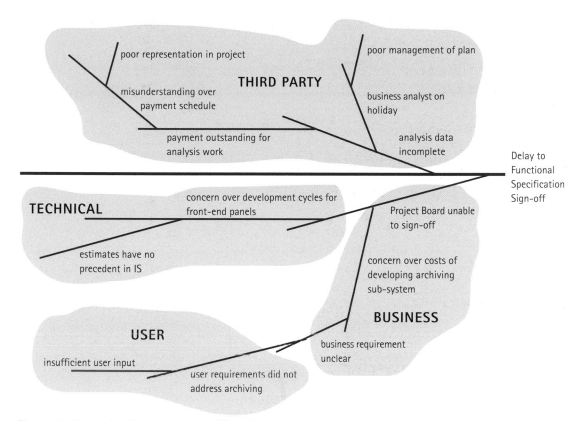

Figure 11: Example of a cause-and-effect diagram

H4   Decision trees

Decision trees are graphical representations of possible events resulting from various decisions. They are particularly useful in weighing the balance between a positive and negative decision.

Construction of the decision tree usually commences from a single premise and works towards a series of possible outcomes.

Figure 12 gives an example of how a decision tree might be constructed to assess the events leading to impact of a dependent project overrunning (i.e. the impact on Project B when Project A overruns). Note that it is possible to calculate separately the probability of each event occurring and express this as a percentage or factor of 1.

In Figure 12, Project B is dependent upon the release of resources from Project A. Project A is overrunning. Depending on the outcome of possible actions relating to the termination of Project A, the probability of the resources being released can be estimated. Note the various actions available which can influence the outcome.

H5   Insurance premium approach

The *insurance premium approach* is useful when a tangible measure of risk significance is required together with a need to prioritise risks. The approach is most effective when providing a measurement of the benefit of risk reduction gained through team consensus in a workshop as opposed to the judgement of an individual.

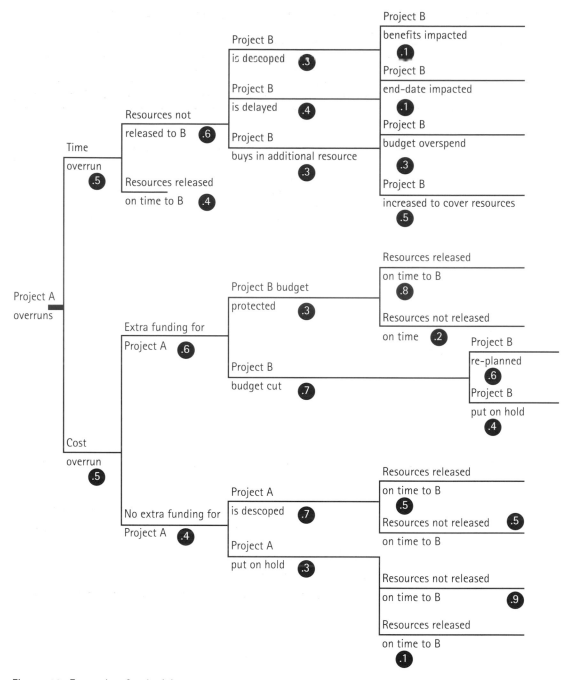

Figure 12: Example of a decision tree

The approach quantifies risk by deciding what insurance premium an underwriter would demand for insuring the risk. The simplest form of calculation to employ is:

CI * P% = IP

where CI is the estimated cost of the risk impact, P is the probability of the impact occurring and IP is the insurance premium.

Table 23: Example of table showing application of the insurance premium approach

Using experienced contract staff versus own inexperienced staff								
RISK	COST OF IMPACT		x	PROBABILITY OF IMPACT		=	INSURANCE PREMIUM	
	Experienced	Inexperienced		Experienced	Inexperienced		Experienced	Inexperienced
Degree of skill								
Higher quality; repair less likely	1.5m	1.5m		20%	60%		0.3m	0.9m
Higher fees; increased costs	0.25m	0.10m		100%	100%		0.25m	0.10m
Staff availability								
Faster completion; less likely to lose benefits this year	1.2m	1.2m		30%	90%		0.40m	1.08m
Degree of control								
Less likely to have a thorough understanding of the business	0.8m	0.8m		70%	30%		0.56m	0.24m
TOTALS							£1.51m	£2.32m

Table 23 looks at the effect on insurance premiums when using experienced or inexperienced personnel.

Three criteria for evaluation have been selected (degree of staff skill, staff availability and degree of staff control). Assumptions concerning each of these have been estimated against the cost of impact and the probability of impact.

The result in Table 23 shows that the insurance premium for the risk is lessened by using experienced staff. A change in data for just one assumption, however, could reverse the result.

H6 Critical Path Analysis (CPA) or Critical Path Method (CPM)

Critical Path Analysis (CPA) or Critical Path Method (CPM) models and associated software are useful for any form of activity planning. The CPA model represents activities using an activity-on-arrow (or activity-on-node) network diagram. This approach is used to identify those activities which are dependent on each other, such as where one activity cannot start until one or more other activities have finished. All activities have assumed deterministic durations. Some activities can take place concurrently in order to identify where slippage will impact or where it will erode some tolerance or require invitation of contingency actions.

Using Programme Evaluation and Review Technique (PERT) models allows explicit modelling of uncertainty in a CPA framework.

H7   Monte Carlo simulation

Monte Carlo simulation is the industry standard for combining probability distributions and forms the basis of most commercial software. It is also the recommended starting point for most IS/IT projects where quantitative risk analysis is required.

Distributions are combined by 'sampling experiments'. For example, a Monte Carlo approach to PERT models involves taking one sample duration for each activity and combining them using a CPA algorithm to determine the overall project duration. This is then separated to obtain a second project duration and so on until there are enough durations to enable a frequency distribution to be established.

Monte Carlo models are highly flexible, but are subject to sampling error. Sampling error can be controlled by using large samples, at considerable cost in terms of computational effort, when accurate results are necessary. Techniques to reduce sampling error may introduce a bias in the results.

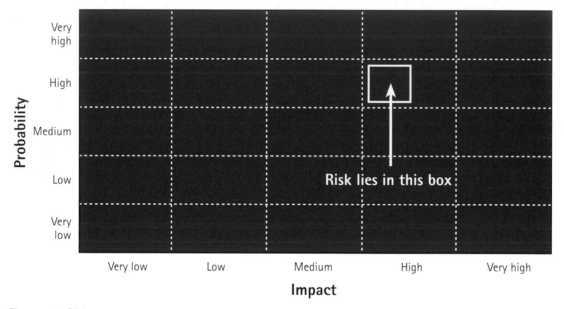

Figure 13: Risk map

H8   Risk map

(Note: this is similar to a Summary Risk Profile but is only for one risk at a time.)

A simple form of qualitative risk estimation requires that the probability of a risk occurring is classified as, at a minimum, 'low (L)', 'medium (M)' or 'high (H)', with a similar classification for the impact if the risk materialises. A combined risk classification of H-H (high probability and high impact if it occurs) is clearly an important risk.

The precise meanings of the classifications must be stated before probability and impact estimations can be made. If this is not done, the terms tend to mean different things to different people.

The ranges should be selected to suit the situation, and take into consideration the business sensitivity. If the qualitative estimates are given explicit meaning in this way, boundaries between these classifications can be drawn to a scale, and illustrated by the dividing lines on a risk map as shown in Figure 13.

H9   Probability and impact grid

Figure 14 shows a grid comparing the probability of occurrence to impact in terms of the number of risks. Qualitative words or quantitative data may be used to label the axes.

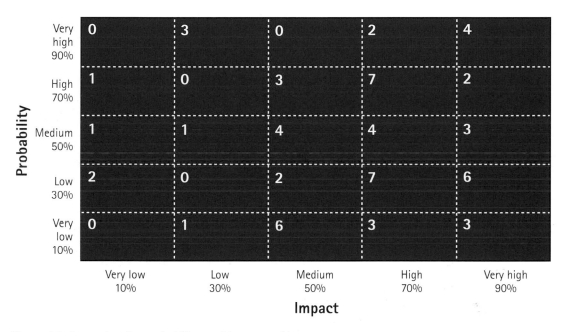

Figure 14: Example of a probability and impact grid

H10   Scatter diagram

A *scatter diagram* can be created using a similar scale to that of a probability and impact grid, but showing concentrations of risk represented by groups of dots. The benefit of such a diagram is to show more visually where the concentrations of risk are greatest. Figure 15 shows an example of a scatter diagram.

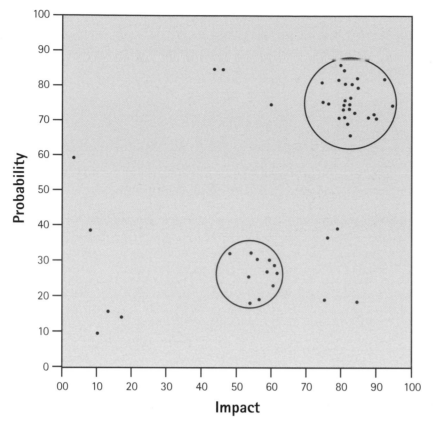

Figure 15: Scatter diagram

H11   Radar chart

Another diagram which has a strong visual impact is a radar chart. Figure 16 shows a typical chart used to show the risk exposure within severity bands by focus area.

H12   Risk indicators

The *risk indicator* (sometimes termed *risk factor*) is the level of acceptability of a risk. Determining the risk indicator is a technique which can be used as part of the risk planning process, prior to evaluation activity.

The purpose of the risk indicator is to answer the question, *Do I want to do anything about the risk?* It can be set as a threshold below or above which appropriate actions may be decided. The risk indicator is thus a filter which ensures that time is not wasted on risks which do not warrant further attention.

The risk indicator is best expressed in terms of cost, for example the cost of doing something about the risk or not, as the case may be. It may, however, be compiled as a combination of time, cost and performance factors. In practice, the business sensitivity of the programme and the commercial environment will provide the necessary information to determine the levels of acceptability.

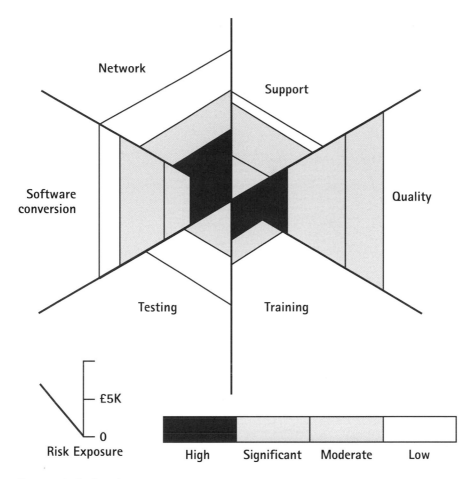

Figure 16: Radar chart

Risks which are deemed to be unacceptable (that is, above the risk indicator), need to be proactively managed. Risks which fall within the limits of acceptability (that is, below the risk indicator) do not require any form of immediate action plan, although they should not be excluded from the ongoing monitoring process, since it is possible that a change of circumstances later result in an acceptable risk becoming unacceptable.

For all risks which do not meet the acceptability criteria, their *degree of manageability* needs to be assessed. In order to do this it is useful to place each risk in one of the following classes:

- unavoidable: nothing can be done to avoid or reduce the risk without changing the nature of the programme/project

- manageable outside tolerance: a course of action could be proposed which would avoid the risk, but this action would have a serious impact on the cost, schedule or other commitments of the programme/project

- manageable: there are one or more courses of action which would effectively reduce the risk

- within tolerance: the likelihood or consequences of the risk, and the cost of these is within the tolerance already accepted for the programme/project.

ANNEX J: LESSONS LEARNED FROM OTHERS

It should be possible to learn from successful projects: how did they make everything work? Typically more is said about unsuccessful ones and so the emphasis tends to be on what went wrong rather than how things could have been done better.

The following extract from an NAO report concerns success.

National Savings and Siemens Business Services (SBS)

This is a high-risk project but SBS considers it is taking a low-risk approach. With 30 million customers, a major failure of the operational service would be a matter of grave public concern. To meet National Savings' requirements and to achieve its expected returns on the project, SBS will have to transform the existing business processes, combined with a significant advance in information technology. These tasks involve a high degree of risk.

Two factors mitigate this risk. First, in contrast with SBS' existing contracts with the Passport Agency and the Immigration and Nationality Directorate, SBS is wholly responsible for new operational processes, supporting IT systems and their use by former National Savings' staff who have transferred under the deal. SBS therefore has more control over this project than on previous occasions, including the cultural change required from its new workforce. If SBS is unsuccessful, it will bear the financial consequences of failure. Second, as there is a system that works and can continue to work until new systems are up and running, SBS plan to change the business processes and supporting IT systems gradually, rather than taking a 'big bang' approach. Each stage, for the most part involving proven IT packages, is to be rolled out well in advance of contracted target dates, and small groups of operations staff will check usability and identify potential improvements.

As the transformation of business processes is central to the success of the partnership, National Savings is monitoring progress through an agreed governance structure and working-level contacts. Alongside this, National Savings has employed independent IT consultants to help it act as an intelligent customer when assessing SBS' proposals and progress.

J1   Assessing success

The first aspect to consider is: How will we know if the project has been successful?

Defining success:

Many observers would regard the Channel Tunnel project as a failure. It was two years late, and costs escalated.

On the other hand, it was a magnificent feat of engineering, and so a technical success. The project was over budget largely because of the intergovernmental safety committee moving the goalposts without monitoring the impact on costs and ensuring ongoing viability. Is it a success or a failure?

A major element of measuring success will be personal, depending on an individual's perception of the project. In particular, different assessments will be made by different interest groups. For a technical development project, you need to consider the perspectives of the following groups:

- **project sponsors (SRO)** will judge the project by whether the end product benefits the organisation, and how much money it saves

- **project managers** will judge their success by whether or not the project was to time, to budget, and to specification

- **technical staff** will concern themselves with the technical quality of the work

- **contractors** will consider whether the project was profitable, and whether it enhanced their company's reputation

- **end users** will judge the project by the effect it has on their working lives: does it make things easier or more difficult?

Sometimes there is little consensus between these viewpoints. A technically sound project may fail to deliver business benefits, and so on.

J2   Why projects fail

Common failings of projects include:

- lack of management structure, people not understanding their role and the responsibility that comes with it, or not having sufficient authority to support the required responsibility level

- inappropriate control of external consultants – lack of clear, unambiguous requirements and means of testing these have been achieved, and/or ambiguity in the contract

- inappropriate pressures of expediency – external pressures dictating what has to be done and the timing which may not be adequately managed in terms of the changes required. It also requires good expectations of management

- failure to understand complexity – what seems to be a 'good idea' at a strategic level may present highly complex cultural and/or technical issues that are not completely understood

- inadequate change control – usually manifests itself as 'scope creep'

- failure to manage business change.

J3   Stopping a project

It can be simpler to let a project keep running. Calling a halt to a project which is heading for failure requires bold decision making by senior management. The project should be stopped if:

- there is no chance of success

- saving it would be at a disproportionate or intolerable cost

- the cost of saving it is greater than the benefit of continuing

- the risks of continuing are too great

- continuing will mean writing off even more investment

- circumstances have changed and the project is no longer necessary

- it is on the wrong track and will be of little benefit anyway.

J4   Barriers

Table 24 summarises the barriers to effective management of risk.

Table 24: Barriers

What are typical barriers to an effective management of risk process?	What incentives can be provided to encourage an effective risk process and support risk taking?
Risk-averse culture	Better recognition and reward schemes for initiative, innovation and well managed risk taking such as stopping a project when required
Lack of culture which appreciates risk and risk management	Removal by top management of the blame culture
A blame culture within the organisation/project etc.	Clear leadership by example
Risk taking is perceived as difficult in the public sector	Encouragement from the Board/senior management
Lack of awareness about management of risk	Better training, involvement and education in risk management
Lack of resources and time	Innovation award schemes, performance bonuses
Lack of training, knowledge and formal risk tools and techniques	Individual accountability for results and achievements
Lack of clear guidelines for staff	An explicit management of risk policy would provide guidelines and ensure staff understand their roles and responsibilities
Uncertainty over funding	Clearly identified authority to commit funding
Absence of a management of risk strategy or policy	Ensure processes are understood as well as ensuring roles are assigned with those with the authority to undertake them

ANNEX K: ASSESSING THE SUITABILITY OF TOOLS

This annex aims to give managers an indication of the things to consider when they plan to adopt a tool to assist in the management of activities.

Chapter 8 looks at techniques to support the various aspects of management of risk. Many of these activities can be supported by tools. Some tools will be general; others will be specific.

General tools may support maintenance of data, for example, a word processor or spreadsheet software may be used to maintain the Risk Register; more advanced spreadsheet software may then be used to generate the Summary Risk Profile for a specific Risk Register.

Some tools support the risk identification and analysis activities and take users step by step through the processes, consider variations in probabilities and so offer a view of a range of possible outcomes which might result from a particular threat.

Other tools provide some support for planning and subsequent management activities.

The following guidance provides general advice on tool selection rather than being specific to management of risk tools, as many of these tools support a wide range of activities, and all aspects, not just management of risk-specific ones, need to form part of the assessment.

K1   Issues to consider when selecting tools

There are a number of issues to consider when selecting and adopting a tool for use within the organisation. These include:

- identifying what you need to achieve and an acceptable cost for its achievement

- having a clear strategy to procurement to support that objective (see Annex E for specific procurement considerations)

- clearly identified method to be applied to the selection and evaluation so that the decision is based on sufficient information to make the objective judgement that can be supported by evidence

- clear statement of what activities the tool is intended to support including details of how and when it will be used

- understanding of the information that will be:

  - available as input to the tool and how this will be provided

  - required as output

- resource implications for undertaking the evaluation and subsequent procurement

- the future resource requirements in terms of:

  - contractual arrangements (will the provider be the only organisation who can provide future training and consultancy?)

  - infrastructure (in particular IT and communications equipment requirements)

- skills and competency requirements of users (in particular for specialist tools: will the tool support people who make periodic use of it, or should there be a dedicated team that are fully conversant with its application?).

K2   Appraisal and evaluation in context

The objective of this section is to define a framework for impartial and effective evaluation to find the product, or products, which best meets the needs and constraints of the organisation.

It is expected that the processes will be used in several ways. The uses include:

- strategic, business-based, evaluation of products to select a 'standard' product for subsequent organisation-wide use

- less detailed evaluation of products as an element of a feasibility study

- full evaluation of products during procurement for a project

- independent appraisal of a product.

There are several issues to be addressed in procuring a tool to support management activities. These include:

- the range of competing products and providers. These bring a wide choice of products and architectures to consider, particularly within the context of competitive procurement policies, and can be confusing for the customer

- the evaluation of software involves understanding the product's capabilities, functionality and limitations, and then organising this information into a coherent framework

- the general lack of an agreed terminology for products

- matching the capabilities of the products against a properly defined requirement.

To make an objective judgement it is useful to take a structured approach to the review of products and their capabilities. This will provide the information required to make the subsequent selection while meeting procurement and organisational requirements.

K3   General appraisal procedure

The overall objective of the appraisal and evaluation procedure is to identify, from all the products that might meet a requirement, those two or three that are the best match. The procedure reduces the number of candidate products through several stages.

This generalised procedure will require tailoring to suit the particular use since the criteria are suitable for many situations. Not all of these activities will be performed in all circumstances, nor will they always be used to the same level of detail.

Having identified the requirement and the criteria against which the selection will be made, the other activities include weighting criteria, identifying products, shortlisting and ranking.

Weighting and planning

The criteria in the resulting evaluation model hierarchy will be of varying importance to the organisation and this relative importance needs to be recorded as weights in the criteria. The justification for the allocation of the weights should be recorded.

The evaluation team should plan how it is to carry out the process of scoring. They should concentrate on those criteria given the highest weighting.

Product identification

Product identification is the process of drawing up of a list of candidate products. If the evaluation is the processing of responses to statement of requirement, then the candidate products are the responses to the document. Otherwise, the potential candidates are those products available on the market.

Familiarisation and shortlisting

The objective of this initial 'shortlisting' is to reduce the list of candidate products to a number that can reasonably be assessed (each of which should be capable of satisfying the essential requirements) without having to resort to detailed technical product evaluation. This whole procedure is one of reducing the list of products on the market down to a shortlist of those that best meet the requirement.

Attending demonstrations is usually only useful for experienced staff, familiar with a range of products, who are able to put what they see into context and ask the relevant questions. It is not usually necessary, or cost effective, to consult technical reference manuals.

Scoring

The shortlisted products are now looked at in greater detail with the objective of allocating a score at the lowest level of criteria in the evaluation model hierarchy. At this stage product demonstrations, discussions with the supplier, reference manual study and reference site visits are usually required.

The assigned scores should be backed up by a set of working notes summarising the considerations that resulted in the scores given. Apart from providing justification for the comparative markings, the notes will prove invaluable if it becomes necessary to review the model at a later stage (e.g. because of the introduction of a new version of a product).

Consider each criteria group at the lowest level. Multiply the weight by the score giving the weighted score.

The process is performed for each product in turn, giving at the end of the evaluation an aggregate score for each product. The list of comparative scores gives the ranking of the products on how well they meet the technical requirements of the evaluation.

High-level view of criteria for software tools

The top level criteria are:

- *functionality* – the knowledge representation techniques and inference methods provided

- *developer interface* – the facilities available to the developer and the skills required for application development using the product

- *integration* – degree to which the product integrates with other software

- *efficiency* – development and run-time machine resource usage

- *development methodology* – degree to which the tool supports any of the emerging methodologies for developing knowledge based systems

- *quality and control* – the facilities available for, and the degree to which it is possible to ensure, high quality software engineering

- *portability* – the range of hardware platforms and operating systems on which the product will run and the extent to which the development environment or individual applications are transferable

- *end user interface* – the facilities available for developing end user interfaces

- *security* – protection of and control of access to data and knowledge and to the tool itself, especially the development environment

- *product credibility* – status of the product and supplier and degree of support, release strategy, training

- *project specific criteria* – other than the above

- *costs* – assessment of direct and ancillary costs; hardware, software, personnel, maintenance, training, development and operation.

It is expected that these criteria, with the exception of costs, will be weighted and scored as suggested earlier. The cost information will be required as an element of the selection procedure, or to exclude products for detailed consideration when they exceed planned budgets or cost ceilings.

K4   Customisation of criteria

The model must be customised to suit specific requirements. This customisation comprises the following steps:

- Alter criteria: the product evaluation criteria are applicable to most projects, yet they may need to be altered in places to meet specific requirements.

- Add criteria: some projects, especially those that are not standard administrative systems, may have special requirements that need incorporating into the evaluation model as additional criteria. An example may be the availability of a library of scientific subroutines for a scientific application.

- Omit criteria: some of the criteria may be irrelevant to a particular project and may be omitted. For example the project may be purely online, and therefore the batch processing criteria are not required.

- Combine criteria: it may be necessary to use all the detail and criteria together and to combine evaluation hierarchies.

- Construct the hierarchy chart: the criteria are arranged in a hierarchical fashion. Each individual criterion is the member of a group that collectively constitutes the higher level criterion. The evaluator(s) should produce a graphical representation of the model of relationships between their criteria.

- Annotate the criteria: it is desirable, particularly if a team is undertaking the evaluation, to annotate the criteria with specific guidelines on evaluation and scoring.

Evaluation teams should guard against the following when carrying out customisation:

- over-simplification – if too few criteria are used then insufficient detail may be gathered and it may not be possible to evaluate products adequately

- appropriateness – the criteria are designed to be generic, so their applicability to the project must be determined in each case

- extensive alteration – the criteria and hierarchies suggested are based on long experience, and as such should meet most requirements. While it is necessary for them to be tailored to reflect the requirements, extensive divergence should be approached with caution.

ANNEX L: DOCUMENTATION OUTLINES

The following outlines describe the purpose of some of the key management documentation which are part of the management of risk process, together with a summary of the typical contents.

L1   Business Case

Purpose: to document why the forecast effort and time will be worth the expenditure to achieve the change and anticipated benefits.

The ongoing viability of the activity can then be monitored against the business case, throughout its lifetime.

Composition

- Reasons for the change (business need and scope)
- Benefits and benefits realisation
- Major risks
- Costs, forecast effort and timescales
- Investment Appraisal (if appropriate).

(Business case needs to cover the strategic fit; business need and scope; possible options with associated cost and investment appraisal; notes on achievability and how this will be assessed; business model and intended approach to acquisition; and affordability.)

L2   Business Continuity Plan (BCP)

Purpose: a plan for the fast, efficient resumption of essential business operations by directing recovery actions of specified teams.

The plan deals with situations of major unforeseeable failures or disasters as well as the continuation of critical business processes. BCP will cover the whole organisation but is likely to be organised as a hierarchy based on location and/or business process such that all or part of the plan can be invoked as required to cope with the situation.

Composition

General introduction and overview, covering objectives, assumptions, responsibilities, how to exercise and maintain the plan

- plan owner
- the plan of response actions to be involved (details following (activity) plan)

- plan invocation – details of how a significant incident is defined and is declared, damage assessment and how to trigger (or prompt) all or part of the BCP

- communications – who should be informed, contact details and key messages (covering key stakeholders and the media). In particular this will include a list of plan holders and details of how they will receive any updates to the BCP

- suppliers – list of any service providers and associated contracts that will be actioned in particular circumstances

- other associated key plans and policy statements (this may include contingency plans, operational risk, security and safety guidelines).

The plan needs to cover the following information, which may be part of the above or separately documented:

- procedures for emergency situations

- fallback procedures

- follow-up procedures

- test schedules (for BCP)

Each of these will cover location, facilities, resources and essential personnel requirements.

More details are covered in Annex F on business continuity management.

L3   Communications Plan

Purpose: to document how information will be disseminated to, and recovered from, all stakeholders in the activity (e.g. project or programme). It identifies the means/medium and frequency of communication between the different parties. It is used to establish and manage ongoing communications concerning the activity. This is a general management product which needs to identify the activity or level it relates to (e.g. a specific project or the strategic level of the organisation).

Composition

- List of stakeholders and their information requirements

- Communication mechanisms to be used (such as written reports, seminars, workshops, videos, e-mails, newsletters)

- Key elements of information to be distributed by the different mechanisms – including frequency and information collection and collation

- Roles and responsibilities of key individuals responsible for ensuring communication is adequate/appropriate and timely

- Identification of how unexpected information from other parties (including stakeholders) will be handled within the scope of the activity.

L4   Contingency Plan

Purpose: a plan that provides an outline of decisions and measures to be adopted if defined circumstances should occur in relation to a specific activity (e.g. project or service).

Composition

The plan (see (Activity) plan), plus

- information concerning the event/incident that is the trigger (or prompt initiation) for implementation of the contingency plan

- plan owner

- details of distribution and storage (showing how people will get a copy of the plan so that they can take the appropriate action)

- resource allocation may be dependent on contracts – in this case details of contracts should be included.

L5   Management of Risk Policy

Purpose: to define how management of risk will be handled within the associated context (could be organisation-wide or for a specific activity such as a project). It covers the lifetime of the activity. It provides information on roles, responsibilities, processes and procedures, standards, tools, facilities and documentation to be produced.

Composition

- View of how processes for management of risk are to be adopted (such that they are appropriate to the size and nature of the context)

- The benefits that management of risk will achieve (within the context)

- Roles and responsibilities for management of risk and ownership of this policy, associated processes and identified risks

- List of standards, required facilities, tools and documentation requirements

- Mechanisms for monitoring application of management of risk

- Criteria and rules for escalation of risk information.

Further information for producing policies for management of risk at the different levels is given at the end of each of the level-specific chapters (Chapters 4, 5, 6 and 7).

Chapter 2 also discusses what is required of a management of risk policy to support the needs of corporate governance.

L6   (Activity) Plans for Programme and/or Project

Purpose: A plan relates to a specific activity (e.g. project). It provides a statement of how and when the objectives of the activity are to be achieved.

It provides the business case with the planned resourcing costs and identified major control (decision) points.

Once approved, a plan acts as a reference against which progress can be monitored.

Note: more details on these plans may be found in PRINCE2 and *Managing Successful Programmes* (see Further Information).

Composition

- Plan description: brief description of the scope of the activity planning assumptions, prerequisites and constraints

- Activity network or overall schedule information

- Information on key (outcomes and/or products) and/or benefits (dis-benefits) expected

- Budgetary information

- Table of resource requirements (requested or assigned)

- Risks and issues.

L7   Risk Register

Purpose: in relation to a specific activity or plan (e.g. project), the risk register lists all the identified risks and the results of their analysis and evaluation. Information on the status of the risk is also included.

These details can then be used to track and monitor their successful management as part of the activity to deliver the required, anticipated benefits.

Composition

- Risk identification number (unique within the register)

- Risk type (where indication helps in planning responses)

- Risk owner raised by (person)

- Date identified

- Date last updated

- Description

- Probability

- Impact

- Proximity

- Possible response actions

- Chosen action

- Target date

- Action owner/custodian (if differs from risk owner)

- Closure date

- Cross references to plans and associated risks and may also include

- Risk status and risk action status.

See Chapter 8 for amplification of Risk Register contents.

L8   Security Policy

Purpose: to provide a definition of security measures to be adopted for the organisation. The security policy must provide clear direction such that all employees, partners and associates can see their own role and responsibility for security. It also provides the metrics within which security measures can be assessed to ensure ongoing adequacy.

Note: further information can be found in British Standard BS7799.

Composition

- Objectives and scope of the policy (a single policy may all aspects of security or may be concerned with individual aspects such as physical security or information security)

- Importance and benefits (goals and management principles) for adopting this policy

- Roles and responsibilities of management, employees and other affected people

- Definition of how security incidents will be reported and handled (processes to invoke)

- Relationship to other policies and guidelines (which may include risk, business continuity, personnel and statutory requirements)

- Ownership of this policy

- Details of how often and what manner this policy is to be updated

- Details of availability (e.g. how will employees etc. be given access, and be kept up to date).

L9   Stakeholder Map

Purpose: documents all parties (individuals or groups) who have an interest in the outcome of the proposed activity. This may include individuals or groups outside the business. For each stakeholder, their interests are identified and the map is used to ensure all their interests are catered for, including keeping them informed and accepting feedback.

Composition

- List of stakeholders

- List of interests (issues that concern them and their attitude towards aspects of the situation which present a risk)

- Matrix of stakeholders to interest.

L10   Summary Risk Profile

Purpose: a mechanism to increase visibility of risk

It is a graphical representation of information normally found in a risk register. It is associated with a specific risk register at a particular point in time.

Composition

- Identification of associated Risk Register and its version/date

- Grid showing probability against impact

- Risk from register plotted (once effects of mitigation have been taken into account).

- Risk tolerance line (showing which risks need information escalating so that decisions can be taken/approved).

See Chapter 8 for further information.

FURTHER INFORMATION

From OGC

Web based products, available from OGC website, include:

- Briefings to support 'Successful IT' including ones on managing risk and the role of the SRO

- *Risk Guidelines* (guidance for managers identifying the 'what' and 'why' for risk management with a focus on public sector concerns)

- *Procurement Guidelines*

- *Gateway Review Workbooks*

Formally published guidance from OGC

- *Managing Successful Programmes* (OGC) – ISBN 011330166

- *Managing Successful Projects with PRINCE2* (OGC) – ISBN 0113308558

- *(IS Management Guide) Managing Change* (OGC) – ISBN 1903091012

From HM Treasury (see HM Treasury website for more information)

- Management of Risk – A Strategic Overview (The Orange Book)

- The Green Book and Little Green Book

- Treasury Taskforce guidance

Other government sources

- Supporting innovation: managing risk in government departments (NAO)

- Successful IT: Modernising Government in Action (Cabinet Office; Office of the e-Envoy)

Details of relevant publications can be found on the following websites:

- OGC at: http://www.ogc.gov.uk/

- HM Treasury guidance can be found at: http://www.hm-treasury.gov.uk/

- Treasury Taskforce, information on PFI, at: http://www.hm-treasury.gov.uk/

- NAO information is available at: http://www.nao.gov.uk/

- Office of the e-Envoy's website: http://www.e-envoy.gov.uk/

Related information

- Parliamentary Accounts Committee IT Projects Report from: http://www.publications.parliament.uk/pa/cm/cmpubacc.htm

- Interdepartmental Liaison Group on Risk Assessment (ILGRA) details at: http://www.hse.gov.uk/dst/ilgra/ilgra.htm

- Turnbull Report on Corporate Governance from the Institute of Chartered Accountants of England and Wales website: http://www.icaew.co.uk/

- APM Risk Management Special Interest Group on Risk – details can be found at: http://www.apm.org.uk/apm/sigs.htm

- Project Management Institute Special Interest Group on Risk – details at: http://www.risksig.com/

- The APM's PRAM guide is available through the APM Group Project Shop – see: http://www.apmgroup.co.uk

- For some current information on tools see the PMI Risk SIG and also the 'Risk Driver' site at: http://www.riskdriver.com/

- *Insight Consulting* – a company managing CRAMM (a risk analysis and management tool) on behalf of the Crown. The company was closely involved in production of the CCTA BCM Guides and offers a wide range of support including on business continuity management and adoption/adherence to BS 7799 (ISO 17799). See their website at http://www.insight.co.uk

Associated standards

List of standards referred to within this guidance – further information is available from:

The British Standards Institute
389 Chiswick High Road
London W4 4AL
Tel: 020 8995 7799
Fax: 020 8996 6411
E-mail: mailto:c_cure@bsi.org.uk
Website: http://www.bsi.org.uk/disc

- BS 7799 (ISO 17799) – this standard provides a comprehensive set of controls comprising best practices in information security.

- BS6079 – this standard provides a definition of project management.

- PD6668 – risk and corporate governance.

- ISO 9000:2000 – this is an international standard concerning processes and controls for the adoption of appropriate quality procedures.

- BS 15000- this standard provides detail on how IT service management can be adopted (processes, roles and responsibilities).

Security

To obtain advice and guidance material on BS 7799 and c:cure, contact:

The British Standards Institute
389 Chiswick High Road
London W4 4AL
Tel: 020 8995 7799
Fax: 020 8996 6411
E-mail: mailto:c_cure@bsi.org.uk
Website: http://www.bsi.org.uk/disc

To obtain general advice on information security, contact:

The Information Security Policy Group Communications and Information Industries Directorate
Department of Trade and Industry (DTI)
151 Buckingham Palace Road
London SW1W 9SS
Tel: 020 7215 1962
Fax: 020 7931 7194
Website: http://www.dti.gov.uk

For information on the UK BS 7799 Users' Group, contact:

The Information Security Policy Group Communications and Information Industries Directorate
Department of Trade and Industry (DTI)
151 Buckingham Palace Road
London SW1W 9SS
Tel: 020 7215 1318
Fax: 020 7931 7194

To obtain publications on information security, contact:

The ISI Business Infoline on 0845 715 2000

Business continuity

- The Business Continuity Institute (BCI) was established to provide opportunities to obtain guidance and support for business continuity professionals. Their website provides a wide range of information on the subject and support for its implementation. See: http://www.thebci.org

- SURVIVE – a business continuity group whose objective is to promote awareness and education in the field of business continuity management and to encourage best practice. See: http://www.survive.com

GLOSSARY

Note: some entries within this glossary are taken from other products either because they make a useful reference or to show where there is a change in emphasis for a specific term based on origin. Reference documents identified in this way are: *Pocket Oxford Dictionary 2001 edition*; *Business Continuity Planning Guide* (BCPG) or *IT Infrastructure Library* (ITIL).

Acronyms list

BCM	business continuity management
BCP	business continuity plan
BCPG	Business Continuity Planning Guide produced by UK Government property advisers (now part of OGC)
BIA	business impact analysis
BIR (BCPG)	business impact review
BSI	British Standards Institute
CEO	Chief Executive Officer
CI	within configuration management will be used to mean 'Configuration Item'. As part of a risk assessment technique could be used to signify 'Cost of insurance'
CPA	Critical Path Analysis
CPM	Critical Path Method
CRAMM	A risk analysis and management method developed by UK Government to protect IT systems/services
HAZOP	a risk assessment method standing for 'hazard and operability analysis, risk registers and databases'
HSE	Health and Safety Executive
IC (BCPG)	incident control
ICAEW	Institute of Chartered Accountants of England and Wales
ILGRA	Inter-departmental Liaison Group for Risk Assessment, secretariat provided by HSE
IP	Insurance premium (value)
IRR	Internal rate of return

IS	information system
IT	information technology
ITIL	The OGC IT Infrastructure Library: a set of guides on the management and provision of operational IT services
LCC	Lifecycle costings
M_o_R	Management of Risk (brand name for this guidance)
MSP	Managing Successful Programmes
N/A	not applicable
NAO	National Audit Office (UK Government body)
NPV	net present value
OGC	Office of Government Commerce, part of the UK HM Treasury
PERT	Programme Evaluation and Review Technique
PFI	Private Finance Initiative
PPM	Project Profile Model
PRINCE2	The standard UK government method for project management that provides a process-based framework for setting up and controlling projects. The acronym stands for PRojects IN Controlled Environments
PSO	Programme or Project Support Office
RAG status	flag that can be used to indicate status of the exposure of a risk. Its status is denoted by colour (Red, Amber, Green)
ROI	Return on Investment
SRO	Senior Responsible Owner
SRP	Summary Risk Profile
SWOT	Analysis of strengths, weaknesses, opportunities and threats within the given situation
WORM (Device)	Optical read only disks, standing for Write Once Read Many

Definitions list

Action owner/custodian	some actions may not be within the remit of the risk owner to control explicitly; in that situation there should be a nominated owner of the action to address the risk. They will need to keep the risk owner apprised of the situation
Asset	*(New Pocket Oxford Dictionary – 2001 edition)* useful or valuable thing or person; property owned by a person or company
Benefits	the positive outcomes, tangible or intangible, that an activity is being undertaken to deliver, and that justify the investment. This should bring about a measurable improvement to existing and new business operations and services
Business case	the rationale for undertaking an activity (project or programme), and justification for committing the necessary resources, setting out the benefits to be achieved
Business continuity management (BCM)	looking at the totality of the organisation: what business services and processes are vital to ensure the business can survive into the future? This includes the derivation and integration of the planning cycle into business operations and the subsequent evaluation of any business continuity measures adopted
Business continuity plan (BCP)	a plan for the fast efficient resumption of essential business operations by directing recovery actions of specified recovery teams
Business recovery plans (ITIL)	documents describing the roles, responsibilities and actions necessary to resume business processes following a business disruption
Change management/control (ITIL)	the processes and procedures to ensure that all changes are controlled, including the submission, analysis, decision making, approval, implementation and post- implementation of the change
Communications plan	detailed plan of when, what, how and with whom information flows will be established and maintained throughout the lifetime of the activity (e.g. programme)
Component	a 'chunk of work' (part of a project) that is to be controlled as a separate entity
Configuration management	the process of identifying and defining the individual (configuration) items in a specific product/outcome; recording and reporting the status of these items and verifying their completeness and correctness
Containment action	an action which lessens the probability of a risk or the consequences and is applied before the risk materialises
Contingency planning	the process of identifying and planning appropriate responses to be taken when a threat (risk) actually occurs
Contingent action	an action that is taken after the risk has happened. Here the focus is on reducing the impact of the risk. These actions can be preplanned and rehearsed before the situation arises
Corporate governance	the ongoing activity of monitoring on a sound system of internal control to safeguard investment and the organisation's assets

CRAMM	a formalised security risk analysis and management methodology originally developed by CCTA (now part of the Office of Government Commerce) in collaboration with a number of private sector organisations
Dis-benefit	an unfavourable outcome as a result of some activity
Disaster recovery planning	a series of processes that focus upon recovery processes, principally in response to physical disasters. This activity forms part of business continuity planning and not the totality
Gateway review	These are independent reviews of major projects in government. They are mandatory and occur at key decision points within the lifecycle of a project
Impact	*(New Pocket Oxford Dictionary – 2001 edition)* a noticeable effect or influence
Incident	*(New Pocket Oxford Dictionary – 2001 edition)* an event
Issue	a concern that cannot be avoided
Management of risk	systematic application of policies, procedures, methods and practices to the tasks of identifying, analysing, evaluating, treating, reviewing and monitoring risk (i.e. incorporates risk analysis and risk management). This provides a disciplined environment for proactive decision making
Management of risk framework	sets the context within which risks are managed in terms of how they will be identified, analysed, controlled, monitored and reviewed. It must be consistent and comprehensive with processes that are embedded in management activities throughout the organisation
Management of risk policy	a product which documents how the management of risk framework will be adopted within a given context (could be organisation-wide or for a specific project etc.)
Maturity level	a well defined evolutionary plateau towards achieving a mature process (five levels are often cited: initial, repeatable, defined, quantitative and optimising)
Operational risk	primarily those risks concerned with continuity of business services
Opportunity	a future event, that should it occur, would have a favourable impact upon the activity (e.g. project)
Partnering	a managerial approach used by two or more organisations to achieve specific business objectives by maximising the effectiveness of each participant's resources
Problem	*(New Pocket Oxford Dictionary – 2001 edition)* something which is difficult to deal with or understand
Procurement	the whole process from identifying a business need to fulfillment of contract. This definition reflects the Gershon Report's wider definition of procurement, which draws in all the activities around ongoing management of a contract throughout its life and the development of long-term relationships with suppliers, as opposed to just the formal processes of arriving at a contract

Product	the output from a piece of work. May also be described as a deliverable or outcome. May be tangible (e.g. a specific document) or intangible (e.g. a culture change)
Programme	a portfolio of projects that aims to achieve a strategic goal of the organisation, planned and managed in a coordinated way
Programme risk	risk concerned with transforming high-level strategy into new ways of working to deliver benefits to the organisation
Project	a specific suite of work aiming at acquiring a specific product or achieving a unique outcome, or series of outcomes, as distinct from being a repetitive process. This will be a temporary organisation that is created to achieve the desired outcome and should be to a specified business case to ensure viability in business terms
Project Profile Model (PPM)	a standard set of high-level criteria against which to assess the intrinsic characteristics and degree of difficulty of a proposed project in order to establish the appropriate control structures, risk profile and corresponding risk strategy and design approach (e.g. use of modularity etc.). Developed by the Cabinet Office (office of the e-Envoy), for use by government organisations (available on the Web). The model should be used to assess the criticality of IT projects and so determine the level of peer review required
Project risk	risks which are concerned with stopping the successful completion of the project. Typically these risks include personal, technical, cost, schedule, resource, operational support, quality and supplier issues
Proximity (of risk)	reflects the timing of the threat of the risk, i.e. is the threat stronger at a particular time? Or does it disappear sometime in the future? Or does the probability or impact change over time?
Residual risk	the risk remaining after the risk response (treatment) has been applied
Risk	(New Pocket Oxford Dictionary – 2001 edition) the possibility that something unpleasant will happen; situation that could be dangerous or have a bad outcome
Risk	(definition as used throughout this guidance) uncertainty of outcome (whether positive opportunity or negative threat) It is the combination of the chance of an event and its consequences
Risk analysis	systematic use of information to identify threats/risks and to estimate the probability of occurrence and severity of the impact and provide information to management such that decisions on optimal responses can be taken
Risk appetite	the amount of risk the organisation is prepared to tolerate (be exposed to) at any point in time
Risk evaluation	the assessment of probability and impact of an individual risk, taking into account predetermined standards, target risk levels, interdependencies and other relevant factors
Risk identification	determination of what could pose a risk; process to describe and list sources of risk (threats)
Risk Log	see *Risk Register*

Risk management	the task of ensuring that the organisation makes cost effective use of a risk process. Risk management requires: processes in place to monitor risks; access to reliable up to date information about risk; the right balance of control in place to deal with those risks; decision making processes supported by a framework of risk analysis and evaluation
Risk owner	A role, or individual, who is in a position to manage the risk and ensure it is controlled. This ownership may relate to specific aspects of the management of risk process or to a specific risk as documented on a risk register
Risk perception	value or concern with which stakeholders view a particular risk
Risk policy	see *Management of risk policy*
Risk process	a series of well defined steps to support better decision making through good understanding of risks and their likely impacts
Risk register	a product used to maintain information on all the identified risks pertaining to a particular activity (project or programme)
Risk response	actions that may be taken to bring the situation to a level where the exposure to risk is acceptable to the organisation. Individual risk responses can be to transfer (some aspects), tolerate, treat or terminate one or more risk
Risk tolerance line	A line drawn on the Summary Risk Profile. Risks on the Summary Risk Profile which appear above this line are those which cannot be accepted ('lived with') without referring them to a higher authority. For a project, the Project Manager would refer these to the SRO
Role	a set of responsibilities, activities and authorisations which can be assigned to one or more people on a full or part-time basis
Security	*(New Pocket Oxford Dictionary – 2001 edition)* state of being secure (certain to remain safe); the safety of a state or organisation
Senior Responsible Owner (SRO)	the single individual (business sponsor) with overall responsibility for ensuring that a project or programme meets its objectives and delivers the projected benefits
Severity of risk	the degree to which the risk could affect the situation
Sponsor, or sponsoring group	the main driving force behind an activity (e.g. project). This will be one or more people representing the appropriate level of management to ensure commitment and authority to the activity is appropriate in relation to its business case
Stakeholder	individual, group or organisation having a vested interest or influence on the business outcome of the activity
Strategic risk	risk concerned with where the organisation wants to go, how it plans get there and how it can ensure survival
Summary Risk Profile	a simple mechanism to increase visibility of risks. It is a graphical representation of information normally found on an existing risk register
Threat	*(New Pocket Oxford Dictionary – 2001 edition)* person or thing likely to cause harm or danger; the possibility of trouble or danger

Threat	*(definition as used throughout this guidance)* a factor that could lead to a risk occurring (i.e. a cause or a risk)
Turnbull Report	report produced in 1999 by the Institute of Chartered Accountants of England and Wales (ICAEW). The report described the needs for appropriate adoption of corporate governance
Vulnerability	*(New Pocket Oxford Dictionary – 2001 edition)* exposure to attack or harm

INDEX

References in *italics* are to items contained in the Glossary.
Fig = Figure. Tab = Table.